D0516122

THE
ARCTIC
WORLD

Marco Nazarri

ABBEVILLE PRESS   PUBLISHERS
New York   London   Paris

The curtain of light that we observe along an east-west arc is the most common form of the aurora borealis.

When the intensity of the phenomenon increases, the light wall begins to undulate and folds back on itself in enormous S-shaped curves, only to once again unfold.

The more energy in the particles from the sun, the more deeply they penetrate the ionosphere and the higher the wall of light becomes; it may reach a height of 300 miles.

Using photometers sensitive to a single type of color, researchers have gained a better understanding of how the aurora borealis works: the pale green and pink colors are produced in the center of the curtain of molecular nitrogen and at the end of the fringe of molecular oxygen, while the red color is produced by atomic oxygen.

As the latitude decreases, the pale green and pink lights disappear and only the red remains. The delicate designs of the fluctuating curtain also disappear, and the aurora borealis becomes an extended reddish glow which is easily visible on a dark night.

We are accustomed to seeing matter in three states: solid, liquid and gas. Plasma is the fourth state of matter in which it is found in the form of highly ionized gas. The aurora borealis is the closest thing to us that manifests as plasma. The phenomenon is thus of great interest, not only as a spectacular sight but also for scientific purposes, and is one of the two planetary puzzles which scientists are currently studying: the other is the now famous hole in the ozone layer.

Another factor that greatly interferes with human activity and hinders many human efforts is the long, winter darkness. However, as "polar humans" do not live exactly on the Pole but at latitudes between 60° North and 80° North, the darkness is never complete, and there is enough light to distinguish objects and the profile of the landscape when the sun is still 6° below the horizon. Even during the shortest day of the year at a latitude of 72° 30', there is still sufficient twilight to move about outside.

The snow cover is a natural reflector which increases the brightness of the weak sunlight. Besides, even when there is no sun, due to the extremely clear winter air, the moon produces enough light to create deep shadows, thus making it possible for people to cross even very rough terrains.

Near the Pole, the moon does not set for two weeks, and even a half moon provides enough light for hunting, traveling and scientific activities. The Arctic atmosphere is thus full of quite varied phenomena and oddities, not the least of which, under many aspects, is the sea.

It is a central element in the Arctic, and everything revolves around it. Research on the sea is at least as important as that of the lands that surround it. Arctic waters cover twice as much territory as the tundra.

In addition, the sea is biologically much more productive than the lands around it. Still, it is primarily of interest because it is different from all other seas.

The most important factor is the great expanse of ice that covers most of it.

This shield at the top of the earth has enormous reflecting power, much more than that of the snowy lands, and can reach 85%-88% of reflection of the sunlight received.

There are basically three types of ice in the Arctic: 1) fast ice that forms around coasts and joins the pack-ice in the summer; 2) pack-ice or drift ice, which is constantly in movement; 3) the polar pack. The last is typical of and found only in the polar sea.

The air temperature in summer barely rises above freezing and is not warm enough to melt the ice cap; the polar pack may thus be many years old. Due to its ability to insulate, it may reach a uniform thickness of about 10 feet, except for a few pressure dikes which form when different ice fields meet and their edges overlap, reaching heights of 18-30 feet.

Given the relatively calm weather conditions of the extreme polar region, this is nevertheless quite rare.

In addition, at these latitudes the ice is quite thick and compact and there are not many open areas which permit much movement.

Drift ice behaves quite differently. It is constantly in motion, with wide areas of open sea among the individual fields, so that encounters with the various frozen surfaces

create true barriers known as hummocks, which are difficult to cross when traveling by sled.

Small ice fields join to form vast fields, then the latter fragment once again or crash into other fields, crumbling into slabs, a few square meters in size, in a succession of movements that continue into late autumn.

In winter even the spaces among the various fields are covered with recent ice, and thus the whole surface looks like a single mass when seen from the air. Finally, polar ice is more resistant and harder than drift ice. Because it is older, the ice has lost almost all its salt, which migrates to the surface in contact with the water. It looks transparent, with tones of green and blue, while recent ice and coastal ice are white and almost opaque.

Their movements are determined by the wind and the constant currents of the Arctic inland sea. Pack-ice drifts at an angle of 25° to 45° from the direction of the wind, at a speed of 1/50 of wind speed.

When the wind is weak or non-existent, pack-ice is carried by the sea current. In Eurasia, the currents move from east to west. The great explorer and scientist Nansen took this fact into account when he intentionally trapped his ship, the *Fram*, in the ice from 1893-96, beginning his drift from Wrangel Island and letting the current carry him, with the goal of arriving at the North Pole.

The drift, however, followed a more southerly route that took him just above the Franz Joseph Land archipelago.

The direction of this drift is nevertheless amply demonstrated by the wood Asiatic rivers carry, which later appears on the coasts of the Svalbard Islands and Greenland.

A branch of the same current runs north of the Svalbard Islands and Greenland, circles Ellesmere Island, heads to the upper Canadian archipelago (the Queen Elizabeth Islands) and runs into the Beaufort Sea. Note also that we can say that the currents in the Arctic Ocean move in a clockwise pattern.

Coastal ice varies greatly depending on the slope of the continental shelf.

On the Siberian coast, which overlooks the largest shelf on the planet, extending for hundreds of miles from the mainland with quite

38 A sunset heralding good weather on little Twillingate Island off the coast of Newfoundland. The photo shows the lighthouse of Crown Point at the northern end of the small island.

38-39 A rainbow arches in a perfect semicircle, while a second one can be glimpsed on the outside. This photo was taken at Wagner Bay in the Barren Lands in eastern Canada.

39 top left A sky full of cumulus clouds is a sign of an atmospheric disturbance that usually does not cause any precipitation. The weather in the Arctic is extremely fickle, however, and the balance between warm, moist currents and cold, dry ones is always precarious.

39 top right Twilight casts a purple hue on the mass of ice accumulated on a section of the Alaska coast. When the sun sets, temperatures plunge to below freezing, silencing the noise of the masses of ice crashing against each other.

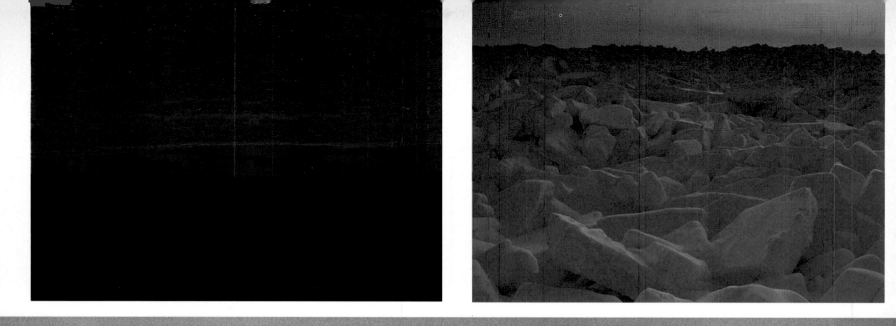

shallow waters, endless fields of fast ice are formed that join with drift ice in the summer. Siberia has many large rivers which remain frozen for eight months of the year, but still dump considerable amounts of warmer fresh water into the sea. While this flow helps melt coastal ice in late spring, it also causes early freezing in the autumn due to the lower salinity of the coastal waters. Similar conditions occur in Canada, where the waters of the Mackenzie River flow into the Beaufort Sea.

A unique feature of the Arctic Ocean is the polynyas, areas of open water surrounded by ice which are relatively stable, even seasonal.

The most well-known are those offshore at the mouth of the Yana River, near the Laptev Strait, and those facing Lincoln Land in northern Greenland. This phenomenon, which is not well understood, is presumed to be caused by the combined effects of prevailing winds and constant currents. Some extremely interesting information on the temperature increase, which affects the Arctic during the summer, has been gained through recent surveys using automatic radio-transmitting buoys, distributed throughout the Arctic Ocean: 2/3 of the temperature increase is due to the sea and 1/3 to southern air currents.

The liquid medium is thus of fundamental importance for the climate of the far North. The mechanism for exchanging the cold, low-salt, surface waters that leave the Arctic and the warmer, more saline, deeper waters that enter it from the Atlantic and the Pacific is shown in the following table:

Inflow		Outflow	
Atlantic	85%	Eastern Greenland current	75%
Pacific	8%	Canadian current	25%
Rivers	4%		
Precipitation/ evaporation function	3%		
==================================			
	100%		100%

The warm and cold currents have a total flow of 6 million cubic yards a second.

How is ice formed? How do lakes and seas freeze? There is a great difference between the formation of fresh water ice and salt water ice. In the former case, the temperature simply needs to go below freezing in order to form a shiny, transparent slab with a thickness which tends to increase if the low temperatures persist. For example, at Lake Baikal one can clearly see fish swimming under a transparent crust of ice one yard thick. Of course, ice formation is facilitated by the absence of waves.

Moreover, ice always begins to form on the coasts and advances toward the center of the body of water, which in turn is the first area to melt as temperatures rise.

In the case of sea ice, the situation is more complicated due to the salt content. Temperatures must drop further and a process begins in which the surface gradually loses salt, which migrates to the bottom, while upon contact with air a mush of salt crystals and ice is formed. Ice forms more easily in river estuaries (less salinity), in calm bays (fewer waves and less wind) and along the coasts, where the high tide is not a significant phenomenon.

As the temperature continues to decrease, the mush solidifies, some of the salt moves farther down and some to the surface exposed to the air, forming a briny mixture of salt crystals and ice that makes the slab non-slippery and opaque. Once it reaches a thickness of 2 inches, the newly-formed slab is quite flexible, able to hold the weight of dogs and sleds. As the slab of new ice increases in thickness during the winter, the process of salt migration continues, especially toward the lower edge, while the upper portion, which is exposed to the snow and wind, becomes increasingly less saline, and the following spring can even be used as drinking water.

If, however, the surface of new ice is broken by a storm with strong waves, the fragments of ice continue to crash into each other, becoming rounded with a pancake-like surface. As brine covers the edges, they begin to look like large water-lily leaves.

This transformation always occurs near the coast, never in the open sea.

With regard to the navigability of the Arctic seas, we should remember Armstrong's words

43 top left The image shows a polar landscape in the moonlight, taken at Scoresby Sound on the east coast of Greenland. Due to the clear atmosphere at high latitudes and the surfaces covered by snow or ice, which act as reflectors, the moon provides enough light for many animal and human activities, making it possible to travel as well as hunt and fish.

43 top right This is the aurora borealis in Greenland. An optical illusion makes it appear as if it is touching the horizon, but the luminous fringe is actually about 100 to 300 miles from the earth.

42 This picture of the aurora borealis was taken at Fairbanks in central Alaska. This phenomenon involves the discharge of an enormous quantity of energy and is caused by a collision of the solar wind, ionized particles that move at great speed, with rarefied nitrogen and oxygen molecules in the atmosphere. Throughout the phenomenon, radio and television broadcasts and electrical energy transport are disturbed.

42-43 A Norwegian coast guard boat crosses the polar waters of Isfjord, the great arm of sea that cuts deeply into Vestspitsbergen Island in the Svalbard archipelago. The city of Longyeatbyenm, the largest in the archipelago, is located on the coast of Isfjord and is connected to Norway by regular SAS flights.

reported in the magazine *Arctic*: "The most important application of the study of sea ice involves the ability to navigate.

"There are other applications: finding a safe place to land for airplanes; finding a route that will support the weight of land vehicles; noting changes in climate for climatologists; and an index for predicting the weather for meteorologists.

"But none of these can match the importance of being able to navigate." The Arctic offers two great itineraries: the Northwest Passage through the Canadian archipelago, and the Northeast Passage along the Siberian coast. Both join the Atlantic Ocean to the Pacific and are alternatives to tropical routes. In centuries past, the Northwest Passage caused sailors the bigger problems (indeed, no one succeeded in navigating the entire route until the great explorer Amundsen's expedition of 1903-1906), and even now it requires the use of special ships with reinforced bows and keels, preferably preceded by ice breakers.

This type of navigation is not very economical, for reasons which include the high cost of insurance, so even today traffic via this sea route is quite rare.

On the other hand, the Northeast Passage, which was first navigated by the Swedish explorer Nordenskjöld in 1878-79, has now been crossed many times, and by the beginning of the twentieth century the voyage could be made within a single year.

This waterway proved to be quite important for the Russians as there were no roads or railways which reached the distant areas of northern Siberia.

After the advent of communism, an ambitious plan was conceived for the construction of an entire fleet of icebreakers, and even today Russia is in the avant-garde of Arctic navigation. It now has over 60 ships of this type, some of which are colossal, nuclear-powered vessels with a tonnage of over 15,000 tons and up to 45,000 HP.

Generally an icebreaker, the size and power of which vary depending on the route it takes, opens the way for a convoy of commercial ships. With the assistance of especially constructed coastal stations to facilitate navigation, ships can now cover the route in less than two months.

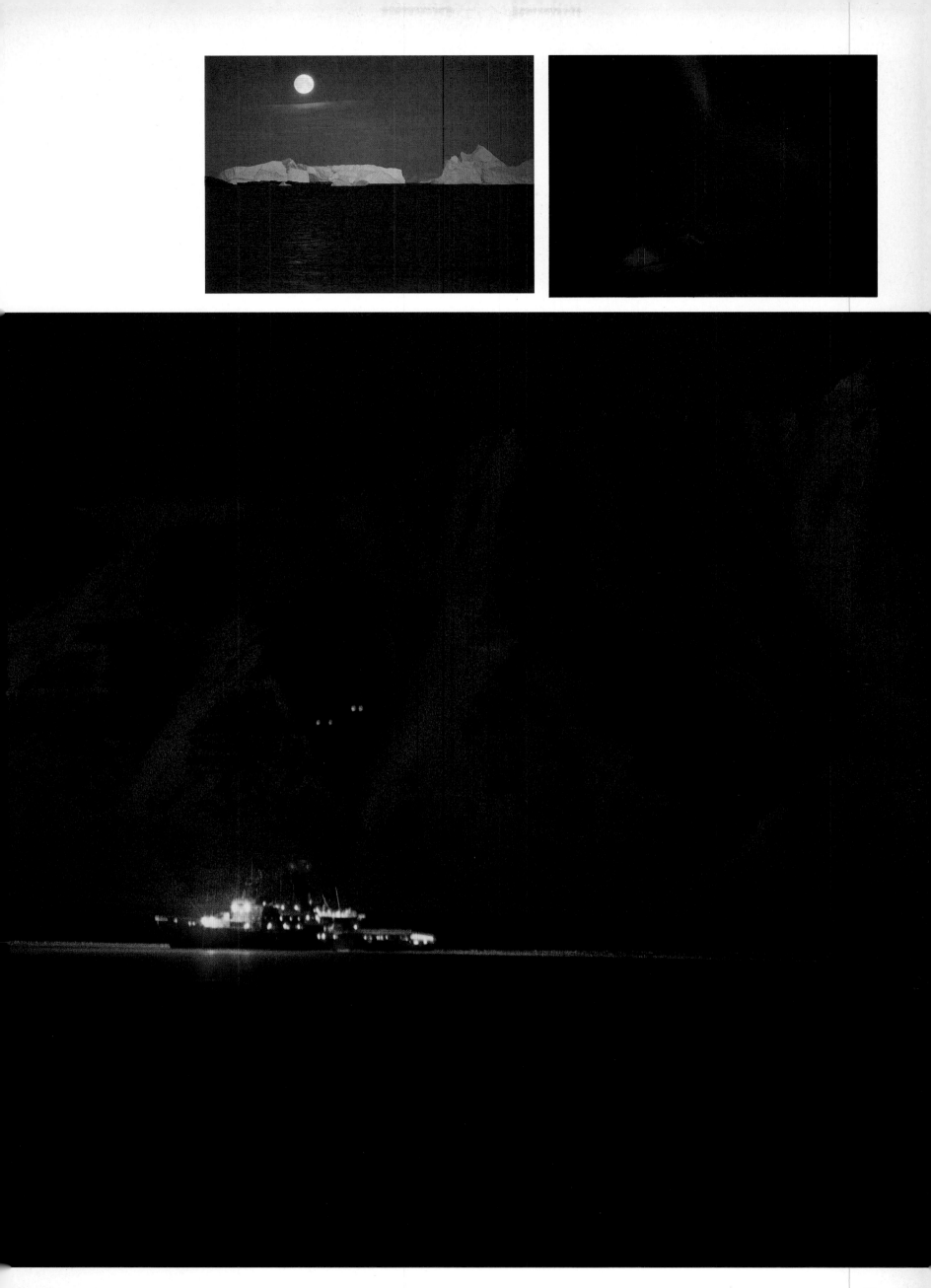

44-45 The aurora borealis is not visible everywhere in the Arctic, only within a fairly regular circle about 1,300 miles in diameter, with the magnetic pole as its center. As the latitude gradually decreases, the green and violet lights and the delicate designs on the luminous fringe disappear. The aurora borealis then diminishes to become an extended clear red glow in the sky.

45 top These two photos of the aurora borealis were taken in Canada. The luminous fringes or curtains are clearly visible. Never still, they move slowly in the sky, sometimes creating S-curves. The different colors are caused by varying amounts of ionized nitrogen and oxygen in both atomic and molecular form. The portion visible to the human eye is only 3-4 percent of the energy emitted; 96-97 percent is energy at infrared and ultraviolet frequencies, which can be detected by means of special instruments.

Indeed, along the Murmansk-Anadyr route there are 12 hydro-weather stations which provide detailed information on ice conditions.

Helicopters provide a complementary observation from both the icebreaker and from bases along the coast. Over the last 40 years the Arctic has become extremely important for commercial polar flights as well. In 1954 SAS opened the Copenhagen-Los Angeles route, which was quickly followed by Amsterdam-Vancouver, London-San Francisco, and Copenhagen-Tokyo routes.

Intermediate stops were Frobisher Bay in Canada or Anchorage, Alaska. With increasingly sophisticated aircraft and the opening of Siberia to international overflights, at present a non-stop Europe-Japan route is possible.

This has made the Arctic one of the most technologically advanced areas on earth, as the installation of radio beacons and extremely powerful radar has created the need for great quantities of electrical energy in addition to specialized personnel. Some of the stations on the DEW (Distant Early Warning) Line set up by the United States during the Cold War years (1952-1957) have been used in Greenland and Canada. This formidable early warning system, which at the time cost 600 million dollars, had already lost much of its military importance with the introduction of intercontinental ballistic missiles and long-term self-sufficient submarines, both equipped with nuclear charges. In the present situation of peaceful coexistence between the United States and Russia, some stations are garrisoned with minimal military staff and civilian personnel. Their support is nevertheless extremely valuable for transpolar crossings.

Nevertheless, the Arctic region's true place in the world's political and economic system is dictated by its incredible wealth of metalliferous minerals and energy resources.

As early as 1856, Greenland exported a precious mineral, cryolite, which is indispensable for the production of aluminum.

This deposit, the only one in the Western world, is located at Ivigtut in southwestern Greenland. In 1894 the Svalbard Islands produced coal utilized primarily for refueling ships on northern routes.

Norway and Russia still mine coal from five different areas. While there are iron deposits on the islands, they do not allow economic independence, yet. There are large coal deposits on Greenland's Disko Island and the Nugssuag Peninsula that faces it. Coal production in such a northerly area was for many years strategic for refueling ships headed to the Canadian archipelago via Baffin Bay, and currently meets the needs of the entire island.

A large deposit recently discovered at Mestervig on the eastern coast is currently producing 20,000 tons a year of concentrated lead and 30,000 tons a year of concentrated zinc, all of which is exported. But Greenland's real wealth is the fishing industry, which has benefited from rising temperatures that have pushed the schools of cod, halibut, salmon, mackerel, sea trout and shrimp, which are in demand the world over, farther north. In 1915 about 20 tons were tinned, by 1950 the quantity had already reached 25,000 tons, and it now is about to reach 50,000 tons.

There are 60 factories that work no fewer than 8-9 months a year, and a large part of the population has concentrated around this industry. A very recent industrial plant also cans surplus mutton not consumed nationally.

But let's turn to Canada, which is indisputably the largest territory.

It still has not been fully explored for resources, but it seems to rival Siberia in its variety of mineral and energy deposits. Like Siberia, Canada's economy began to develop with the trade of furs, at that time 100% dependent on the activity of indigenous peoples.

The white foxes of the tundra and muskrats in particular were captured at the mouth of the Mackenzie River.

In the 1920's revenues came to 300,000 dollars for fox and 2 million dollars for muskrats. Other animals, including bears, wolves, wolverines and lynx, accounted for much less.

At that time, the export of furs was the country's third largest economic activity.

The skins of caribou and seals had always been used locally more than anything else, and the fishing industry, Canada's second largest business, was concentrated at lower latitudes around the islands of Newfoundland.

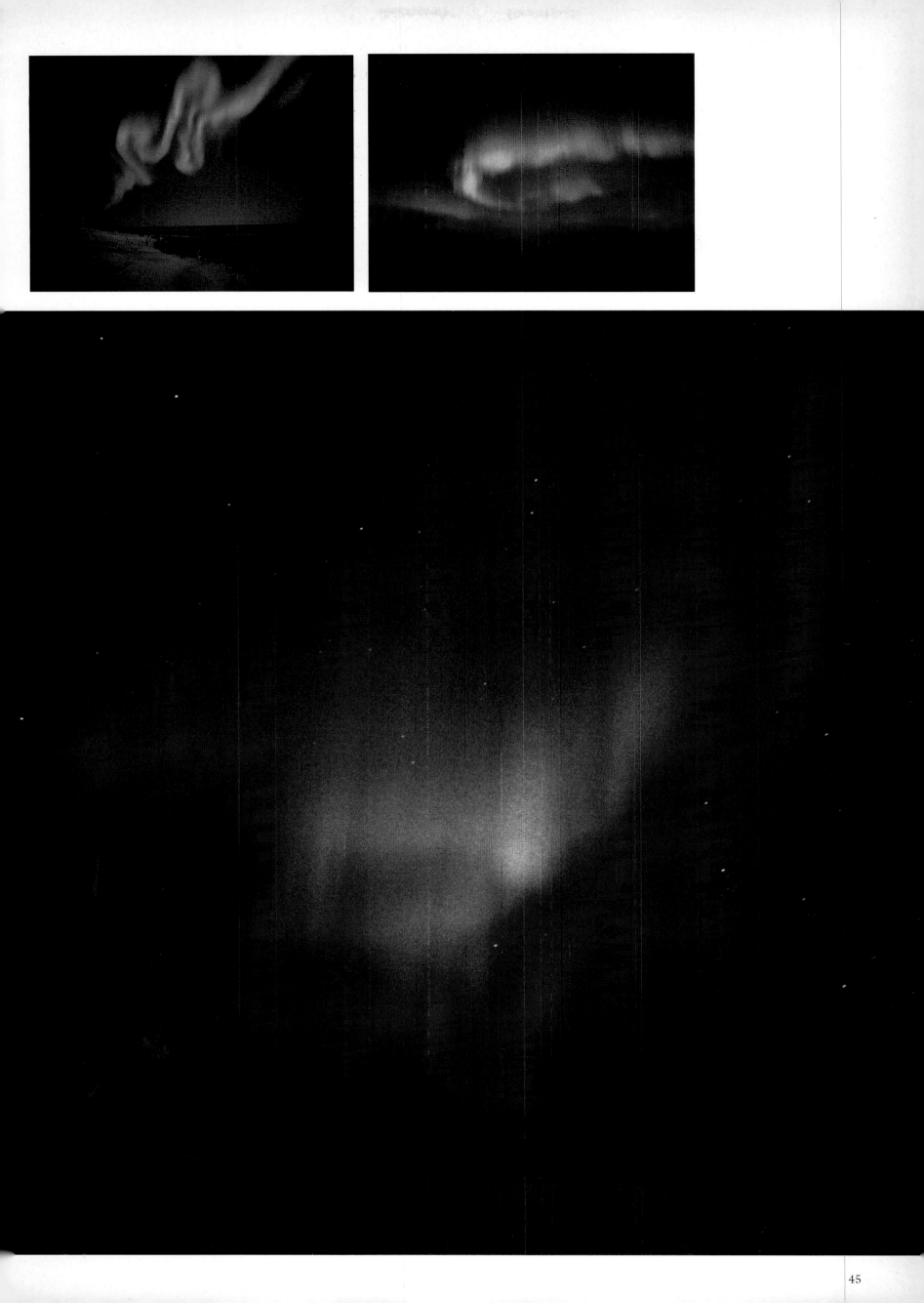

46 top left A volcanic eruption taking place in the middle of the great Vatnajokull glacier in Iceland, a group of extinct and active volcanic cones covered by a thick layer of ice that extends for over 5,000 miles.

46 top right In late spring, a section of the coast in the Svalbard islands is still blocked by land ice, the first to form in the autumn and the last to disappear in the summer.

The primary source of income at that time was the export of timber, especially to Japan and the United States.

The discovery of gold along the Klondike River began the mining age, and a rather rich but small vein was tapped. The later discovery of other metalliferous deposits proved to be much more important, with about 25% still in activity. A mine is already operating full-time at Rankin Inlet, where the mineral deposits contain copper mixed with zinc. On the northern part of Baffin Island there are deposits of platinum, gold and silver, while on the Ungava Peninsula there are deposits of copper and nickel.

There are copper deposits at Coppermine and on Victoria Island. Ferrous minerals are located in various areas: the Belchers Islands, Baffin Island and the Ungava Peninsula, which is considered the most important deposit in North America. There are large uranium deposits at Uranium City, while 50% of the country's gold is mined at Yellowknife.

Finally, perhaps one of the most important discoveries is that of the oil and natural gas fields in the province of Alberta and at the mouth of the Mackenzie River, where a new city, Ivigtut, has grown up; it will probably become the northern terminal for the oil pipeline running to Prince Rupert via Whitehorse.

But the most feasible project being studied is an underwater oil pipeline which would join Melville Island and Quebec, skirting Baffin Island and Labrador.

At present, about 50% of industrial investments are in the oil industry. Alaska's economy has also long been tied to the fur trade, the timber industry and fishing. Even today, during a year, 70,000-80,000 fur seals are officially killed at the Pribilof Islands, while the salmon canning industry is quite important. As in Canada at Frobisher Bay, over the past 20 years enormous frozen fish factories have been built; the fish is exported in its natural state and is then smoked at its place of destination.

In Alaska as well, mineral exploitation began in 1899 with the discovery of gold at Nome. In a short time the deposit produced 100,000 dollars worth of gold, and a small amount is still mined even today.

46-47 This great iceberg comes from the east coast of Greenland; its geometric formations, still untouched by the waves and weather, show that the mass of ice is of quite recent origin. During the summer, mostly due to the wind, icebergs move faster than the broken pack-ice that surrounds them, while in the winter the frozen sea obstructs all movement.

47 The Peel River runs through the westernmost part of the Northwest Territories. The river arises in the Yukon and then flows lazily across the great flatland that includes the delta of the Mackenzie River, into which the Peel flows. The photo clearly shows the flat, marshy character of the region, due in part to the permafrost that prevents drainage.

48-49 Roald Amundsen, the great Norwegian explorer, was the first to complete the difficult Northwest Passage in the small Gjöa in 1903-1906. During the journey, the Norwegian was blocked for months by the thick pack-ice, but took advantage of the adverse conditions to explore the region on foot, determining the location of the magnetic North Pole and discovering that it moved every year. After his extraordinary expedition to the South Pole, which he reached in 1911, he made a series of expeditions to the Canadian Arctic that lasted fully seven years, from 1918 to 1925. Despite the skill of Amundsen and his crew, the ship Maud succumbed to the ice at Cambridge Bay on Victoria Island, not far from the Canadian coast. The remains of the ship are still where it was abandoned. The photo on the left shows a portion of the deck and a windlass, the top right one shows the bilge pump, and the other two images show other details of the ship.

There is an important tin mine along the coast of the Bering Sea not far from Cape Prince of Wales. It is particularly valuable because it is the only source of this metal in the United States. A curious fact: Russia also has a single tin mine at the same latitude.

On Seward Peninsula there are large deposits of uranium and tungsten, both of which are strategic metals. Good quality coal can be found at Meadow River, and in the past it was utilized to refuel ships heading to the Canadian archipelago. Extremely important deposits of copper are in the same area of the Kobuk River. But once again as in Canada, the raw material which completely changed the face of Alaska is natural gas and oil.

Even before beginning production at Prudhoe Bay, where so much oil is produced that it requires its own oil pipeline running almost 800 miles to Valdez and the southern part of the country, there were large fields tapped at Point Barrow, Gubik and Umiat, with reserves estimated to be several ten of millions of barrels (each barrel is about 31.5 gallons).

When the Prudhoe Bay facility went into operation the reserves increased: they now come to 80 billion barrels of oil and 15 billion cubic yards of natural gas. Finally, 22 billion tons of fossil coal are produced. Mining and drilling in the Arctic meet one quarter of the needs of the United States, which consumes 60% of world production.

To complete the picture of this state's rapid development, Alaska leads the Arctic in tourism and local handicrafts. The state that claims the 49th star on the American flag is this great North American nation's last true frontier. Its natural beauties are still basically intact, fishing and hunting possibilities are endless, and visitors to the state interested in mountain climbing will find the highest mountains and largest glaciers in America right at hand.

Apart from guided tours, a trip to Alaska is still an adventure with its vast expanses of wilderness, its myriad wild animals, and its Eskimo and Indian tribes which proudly and stubbornly continue to live and hunt according to their ancient traditions. Recently a new and singular opportunity has been added that makes a trip to this state even more special: with no

50 The on-board helicopter has left a group of researchers on the pack-ice to take some scientific measurements.

50-51 The image shows the Russian icebreaker Sovietskyi Soyuz, one of the most modern of this type of nuclear-powered ships. In 1995 this heavy ship sailed up to the North Pole, with several foreigners on board as well. Like all units operating in the Arctic, all of the icebreaker's on-deck works are painted red to improve visibility.

51 top left A detail of the bow is shown, with three rafts ready to be dropped into the sea.

51 top right The icebreaker opens a wide channel in the ice for the ship following it.

formalities, within an hour's time visitors can travel to the Chukchi coast, where the inhabitants have quickly learned to speak English and produce much better quality crafts than those sold in Alaska.

In the spring dogsled races across the frozen Bering Sea are already being organized, and on the Chukchi coast the dollar has now become the tutelary deity of a new wealth. Tens of private airplanes from Alaska, often full of dogs and sleds, touch down on the landing strips every day, especially at Eulen and Providenja. The exciting runs and refreshment areas that local inhabitants have prepared are greatly appreciated by American mushers, who just can't seem to find enough room in Alaska to practice this sport.

Tourists visiting Alaska are nearly all American, while 20% are mainly Japanese, followed by Australians, Germans, New Zealanders and visitors from other Asian and European countries. While a fistful of dollars brings joy to Alaska's neighbors across the road, it would take much more capital to exploit all of Arctic Siberia. This region certainly has just as much timber, mineral and energy resources as the North American Arctic, but at present it lacks sufficient capital.

In the Asiatic Arctic as well, the basic economy has always been typical of the far North: hunting, fishing, mining and reindeer-breeding. Coal was once more important than other minerals, as a coastal deposit was essential to refuel ships along the North-East route. Even after it sold Alaska to the United States, Czarist Russia was a world leader in fur trading. Until the mid-19th century, 1/3 of Russia's national income came from fur sales, and even today Russia is the world's leading producer of furs.

Fishing also has ancient origins. Great processing plants are located in Murmansk, at the mouths of the Ob and the Ienissei rivers, while both fish and giant Pacific crabs are caught near the Chukchi Peninsula and Kamchatka and then exported all over the world.

While cetaceans and pinnipeds can now only be hunted by the local populations, reindeer-breeding is still common inland, and the country's approximately 4 million reindeer are

a true national heritage. Reindeer breeding has increased the value of the land, as it is not yet feasible to practice agriculture here.

Another good source of income is the sale of timber, 90% of which takes place through the port of Igarka on the Ienissei River and 10% through Pacific ports. The main destination is Japan, with some timber sent to Korea and Australia as well.

But all of these activities together are not worth even 1/10 of the mining and energy industry. When the communist regime came to power in the 1920's, it advocated a nationalistic, autarchic policy in which the Soviet Union was to become self-sufficient for its domestic needs, avoiding political and commercial contacts with other nations as much as possible.

Thus, a colossal plan for a geo-mineral survey of the immense territory east of the Ural Mountains was put into action (this gigantic undertaking can be considered still in progress today). The most promising district seems to be the Chukchi Peninsula, where lead, zinc and copper are abundant.

Gold mined from the basin of the Anadyr River near Markovo already accounts for half of Russian production. Moreover, the only tin deposits in Russian territory are on the coast of the Chukchi Sea. This metal is associated with another extremely valuable element, tungsten, while uranium, another strategically important metal, is found in large, still untapped deposits on Komsomolets Island in Severnaya Zemlya. At present it is more economical to process the mineral at Lovozero on the Kola Peninsula, with deposits estimated to be the largest in the world. Not far from Lovozero there is also a large deposit of nickel, whereas in the Urals there are large quantities of lead, zinc and copper.

The same elements were recently discovered in Novaya Zemlya, which is a geographical continuation of the Urals, and mining for them has begun. Nevertheless, the richest, largest deposits of all are in the region around Norilsk, a new city that seems to have sprung up out of nowhere, with platinum, cobalt, nickel, copper and a deposit of high quality coal as well. Another nickel mine is located at Petsamo, in

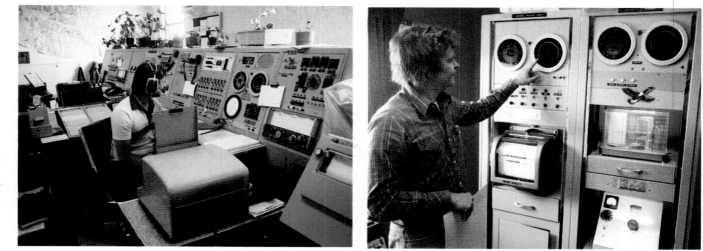

55 top The photos show some of the equipment used to study atmospheric phenomena in the Arctic. The laboratories were installed by the United States and Canada at Resolute Bay on Cornwallis Island, not far from the magnetic North Pole, which is offshore from neighboring Bathurst Island.

56 top The Transalaska
pipeline, here shown near
Fairbanks in central
Alaska, connects Prudhoe
Bay on the Arctic Ocean
to Valdez on the Pacific
Ocean. The pipeline is
almost 1,000 miles long
and crosses two large

mountain ranges and
over 800 waterways. The
pipe is almost four feet
in diameter. The pipeline
was also specially buried
or elevated in areas
where it crosses the
migratory routes of the
caribou.

formerly Finnish territory that was ceded to
Russia after the Second World War.

In addition to Norilsk, large quantities of
coal are also found at Vorkuta, a city on the
railway line that connects Moscow to the
mouth of the Ob, and other mines are
scattered all along the Arctic band.

The basin of the Pechora River has not only
one of the largest coal deposits, but at Ukhta
there is also a considerable source of natural
gas and an oil reserve which has not yet been
calculated. A gas line from the Ustpost field on
the Ienissei River brings methane to the heart
of Western Europe, including Italy.

Great gas and oil reserves have been
prospected on the continental shelf, which with
its shallow waters and extraordinary length
promises to pose fewer technical difficulties
than production on land with its permafrost.

To offset the uncomfortable climate, the
long winter nights, and the difficulties in
communicating by sea and by land, the Arctic
seems to offer humans a cornucopia of
precious, often unique materials which are
indispensable for running the great industrial
machine which they have built in the temperate
regions. Unfortunately, the race to shift the
boundaries of human activity ever farther
north, as occurred after the last war, has had its
effects on the environment, which had
remained isolated and intact for millennia and
is now suffering its first wounds.

Tragically, these wounds seem impossible to
heal. In some cases, mechanical obstacles which
block the free movement of animals have been
created. One example is the Alaskan pipeline,
which in some areas had to be elevated or
buried to avoid interfering with the migratory
routes of the caribou. The oil platforms off
Point Barrow located on the route that
cetaceans follow in the spring to reach
Beaufort Sea make noises which could interfere
with the whales' delicate orientation system.
There has been a great increase in naval traffic
in Lancaster Sound, where most beluga whales
and narwhals come to gather and reproduce.
Further damage occurs when an accident or
improper maneuver causes oil spills from
tankers crossing the sea.

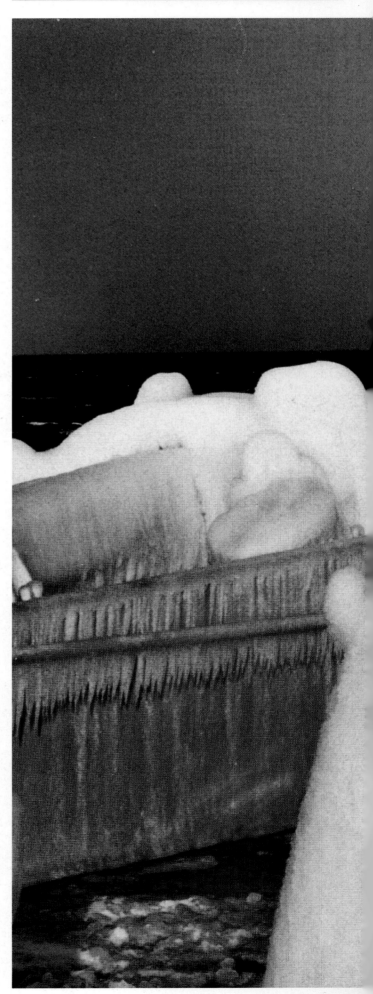

56-57 This is an example
of the severe weather
conditions ships may have
to endure on the North
Pacific route. The ship
Vega Seal is transporting
coal to China and Japan
from the port of Seattle
in the United States. It
has encountered high seas
off the Kurile Islands,
and the low temperatures
have caused splashing
water to freeze on the
deck, forming walls of ice.
At higher latitudes, not
only the deck but the
entire works are covered
with ice during storms. It
does not take long for
dozens of tons of extra
"cargo" to accumulate,
and if this ice collects
over the ship's center of
gravity it can jeopardize
its stability.

57 top left A deposit of
raw minerals at
Nanisjvlk on Baffin
Island. Pictured are lead
and zinc, but the island
is also full of precious
metals like platinum,
gold and silver. The
minerals are loaded onto
ships during the brief
summer/fall season and
are then processed in
Canada's southern
provinces.

57 top right This is Seal
Island, one of the three
artificial gravel islands
constructed for oil
drilling off the Alaskan
coast in the Beaufort Sea.
In just one year the
island was built and oil
rigs were installed, and
by 1985 Seal Island was
already in operation.

The accident that caused 38,000 tons of crude to be dumped into Prince William Bay in Alaska is now sadly famous. It caused the deaths of tens of thousands of marine mammals and an incalculable number of birds. Even on the mainland, the advancement of human communities ever farther north brings the problems of waste with it. These wastes are practically indestructible due to the low temperatures and the lack of bacteria that decompose organic substances. Piles of waste have become a sad, man-made part of a landscape that only a short time ago was still pristine.

Wastes have also become supermarkets for white bears, dozens of which gather near the town of Churchill on Hudson Bay. They then have to be anesthetized and transported farther north by helicopter. Yet the most subtle danger does not come from the lands inhabited by Arctic animals, but from much farther away, with pollution of the sea caused by chrome and mercury from industrial wastes. Air pollution is caused by numerous chemical compounds, primarily pesticides and herbicides. These substances are transported by high altitude winds blowing toward the polar regions and are absorbed first by the plankton, which is then eaten by larger animals like mollusks, crustaceans and fish, and ends up in the blood of mammals, where the concentration can vary from 1000 to 3000 times the initial rate.

If strict controls are not placed on products used in agriculture and emissions of industrial fumes, pollution in Arctic regions will reach lethal doses, with grave consequences not only for animals, but for humans as well.

A recent confirmation that contaminating substances can be carried for long distances came with the radioactive cloud that escaped when the Chernobyl nuclear power plant malfunctioned: the most serious consequences occurred thousands of kilometers away in Lapland, where in Sweden alone 40,000 reindeer had to be slaughtered because the dangerous levels of radioactivity in their bodies made it perilous to eat them and would have had negative consequences on their offspring as well.

58 top left The two photos show two explorers as they cross the pack-ice on their way to the North Pole. Note the extremely rough terrain and the high pressure dikes, caused by collisions of different banks of ice. Along with the wet snow, which prevents runners from sliding, these dikes are the major obstacle along the route, as they could collapse at any moment and damage the sleds as they cross.

59 top During a cruise to the Svalbard Islands, tourists cross Hinlopen Sound on foot. This arm of sea separates Vestspitsbergen Island from Nordaustland, and crossing it in the summer is one of the thrills an organized cruise offers visitors.

58-59 A skidoo, or snowmobile, pulls a sled near Pond Inlet on Baffin Island. This is on the northern coast of the island across from Bylot Island, both of which are part of the Canadian archipelago. Gigantic icebergs are still imprisoned by the pack-ice in May.

60-61 An impressive array of icebergs rises up in Scoresby Sound in eastern Greenland. At almost 200 miles long with various branches, this fjord between the 69° and 70° parallel north is the longest in Greenland. The icebergs all come from the great Dauggard-Jensen glacier on the western end of Scoresby Sound.

A WORLD OF ICE
AT THE END
OF THE EARTH

Two different aspects affect the extreme northern lands: the first is the absence of vegetation (which makes it possible to travel long distances without meeting natural obstacles, as happens in the deserts at other latitudes) and the presence for a large part of the year of snow covering everything, hiding details of the land, in particular the coastal profile and the presence of rivers and lakes, leveling everything under a monotonous mantle of white.

The Arctic's present-day appearance is due to various phenomena: glaciers in the remote and recent past, the permafrost, or frozen ground beneath the surface, and ice both on the mainland and in the sea. For the time being, we will limit our discussion to a particular formation

of ice which looks like an extension of the mainland and may be considered a part of it. It is known as an ice-shelf. Unlike the gigantic shelves in the Antarctic, ice shelves in the Arctic are rather small.

They look like offshoots of land that extend into the sea, and are noticeable due to their size, which can reach 45-65 feet above the flat surface of the pack-ice. They are not formed by the land glaciers that flow into the sea, which produce icebergs composed of freshwater ice and often carry morainal materials with them.

A number of physical parameters, including temperature, currents and degree of salinity, contribute to the formation of these true islands of plate-like ice. Very significant examples of these formations, which adhere to the mainland

and can begin to break off after a few years, drifting imprisoned by the pack-ice, are found in the northern part of Ellesmere Island. Unlike the great Antarctic plate-shaped platforms, which are perfectly flat, those of the Arctic have undulations parallel to the coastline. In summer, melted ice fills the hollows, which increases the height of the undulations over the years.

Another phenomenon found in the Arctic is snow dunes. At high latitudes the snowfall has a density which, with a dry climate, makes it so the wind can shape the snow and form dunes which look quite similar to the sand dunes formed in deserts. Unlike sand, snow will agglomerate and stick together, so that once they have been formed by the wind, snow dunes tend to solidify and can bear the weight of human beings.

There are many of these formations on the flat coasts of Alaska and Canada, as well as along the long Eurasian coast. The wind tends to carry the snow away from the hills and transport it to valleys and earth cracks.

This causes a great accumulation which may become several yards thick and will remain unchanged until the summer thaw.

As the snow rapidly melts, it forms streams which become impassable torrents in July, only to completely dry out in autumn. Signs of past erosion caused by ice are still evident today, as are signs of sedimentary deposits.

One might think that the presence of great masses of ice from a few inches to a few yards thick would have left clear marks on the land, but this is true only if the slope of the land caused the movable mass of ice to slide downward, leaving its mark on the rocks it passed and carrying the material it gradually picked up down to the bottom.

In this case, the traces which we still see today are extensive morainal amphitheaters. An examination of the materials transported tells us something about the first, long-ago cores of the glaciers and the size and duration of the glaciation.

Of course, as noted above, the absence of forests makes it easier to observe the phenomena of erosion and depositing.

But if the territory affected by the accumulation of ice was originally flat or almost flat, as is the case in most of the Arctic, there will be few noticeable signs of it today, except for two

62 The image shows a winter landscape on Ellesmere Island on the northern edge of the Canadian archipelago. The wind has shaped the snow into fantastic forms, changing the landscape's appearance. The low temperatures freeze the snow sculptures into place —until the next blizzard.

63 The March sun on Ellesmere Island has already exposed some of the land, aided by the wind that blows more intensively on higher areas and by the scarce snowfalls.

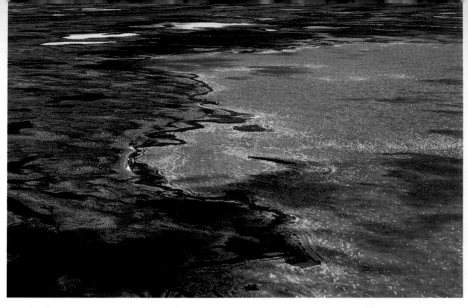

64 top *The coast of Victoria Island in Coronation Bay, in the Canadian Northwest Territories, was photographed in summer, when the tundra vegetation extends to the sea.*

64-65 *This glacier in Alaska is shown from the seaward side. Crevasses are created by differences in the rocky base as well as heavy rain brought in by moist Pacific air, softening the ice layer.*

65 *This picture of the coast of Baffin Island, which is part of the Canadian archipelago, shows some interesting details: rivers and freshwater lakes are still frozen, while the sea is ice-free. Coastal sea ice is still present; it is the first ice to form in the fall and the last to melt in the summer.*

phenomena: the elevation of the ground (still in progress), which reacts flexibly to the great pressure exerted and tends to reassume its original position; and the presence of eskers, which are traces of glacial rivers that flowed beneath the frozen cover.

The materials carried downstream with moraines and those that form eskers are generally coarser in texture, comparable to rocks and rubble, but erosion has also produced a large quantity of powdery boulder clay, which is deposited and pressed by the ice to create characteristic formations known as drumlins, which look like large, half-buried pipes with their axis paralleling the direction the glacier flowed.

This is not true of the mountainous areas where the ice sculpted the territory more powerfully. At the summit we can see Alpine-type ridges and spurs which lie on walls lifted by the ice, with the actual valley at the lower edge, covered with sediment.

The whole structure has the characteristic U-formation that distinguishes glacial valleys. Where these extend out to the sea, they create fjords, which are actually deep glacial valleys which were filled with water when the sea level rose and which are generally shallower at the mouth due to the presence of morainal accumulations from the distant past.

Many Arctic regions have impressive fjords; they appear in Novaya Zemlya, in the Svalbard Islands, in Greenland, in the eastern Canadian islands and in Labrador.

Scoresby Sound in Greenland and Admiralty Inlet on Baffin Island are two of the longest fjords in the world. After examining the physical transformations, which primarily involve the superficial action of ice on the land, it is important to study the part of the Arctic that is an endless flatland, bounded to the north by the coasts of the Arctic Ocean and to the south by the timberline.

This region is known as the tundra, an ancient word of Finno-Ugric origin, and extends to the northern edge of the continent of the northern hemisphere, covering an area about 5 million square miles in size, approximately 1/10 of the planet's land above sea level. The tundra has a harsh climate almost all year round, and it is mostly barren, beaten by northerly winds which

find no great obstacles. Despite these unfavorable influences, when the blanket of snow melts during the summer colorful flowers bloom and the land is full of life, attracting numerous migrating species. Even in winter it provides a refuge for a number of sedentary species. During the long Arctic nights and the short winter days, the area receives very little heat. Only with the return of the long summer days does the warmth succeed in melting the layer of snow and thawing the surface layer of earth. Below, at a depth of one yard or a little more, the earth is always frozen. This phenomenon is known as permafrost, and it may reach a depth of over 300 feet or more, depending on the nature of the land. It occurs exclusively in the tundra.

Permafrost may be continuous, intermittent or sporadic, and may push far south, affecting the taiga, or forested area. It also creates enormous problems in construction work, making it necessary to use special and often extremely costly measures to avoid buildings tilting, sinking or even collapsing. Everyone knows that the far North is cold, but not everyone knows how arid it is; only a little over 7 inches of snow and rain fall on the tundra annually, about the same amount that falls in the desert. For this reason the tundra is often referred to as a "cold desert", but unlike other deserts the tundra retains its water both because the cold air cannot easily carry water vapor and because the solid barrier of the frozen subsoil prevents water from dispersing into the ground. Consequently, drainage problems throughout the tundra are extremely difficult to resolve.

66-67 These icebergs were photographed in southeast Alaska, where the two narrow arms of sea at Endicott and Tracy come together. This area is part of a nature reserve south of Juneau, the capital of Alaska, an hour's sail on the Stephen Strait. Note that the ice is old and transparent, with almost no air bubbles. The icebergs were shaped primarily by the rain, which falls more heavily here than anywhere else in Alaska.

68-69 This photo was taken in Lancaster Sound in the Canadian archipelago. Summer has already arrived, and little remains of the pack-ice that completely covered the sound in the winter.

70 *As the ice-pack breaks up, this block of ice has broken off into a strange sickle shape. This is in the Prins Christian Strait on the southern tip of Greenland, on the eastern coast.*

71 *This iceberg off the southern coast of Greenland has taken the form of a sailboat with unfurled sails. The various marks on the walls of the iceberg show that the mass of ice has changed its hydrostatic position a number of times.*

72-73 This impressive
image shows an arm of
Jakobshavn glacier in
Greenland. Recent
satellite reports show that
it is the most prolific in
the world. It dumps an
incredible quantity of
25,000 tons of ice a day.
The glacier has an
ablation front about
2500 feet in size and
moves at a speed of
almost 100 feet a day.

74-75 This was taken at
Krossfjord in the far
northwest of
Vestspitsbergen Island in
the Svalbards. A late
snow covers the brilliant
flowers of Silene acaule, a
type of moss that grows in
dry, rocky soil.

the flora in this region, we should take a look at the individual regions, each of which has its own, sometimes unique, characteristics.

In a way this is similar to going from theoretical to applied morphology, as it can be seen that even though they have the same climate and latitude, these regions vary greatly from place to place, making it impossible to understand them through a general description.

Recalling the definitions and conventions noted in the introduction, the following regions can be considered Arctic, starting from Europe and proceeding counter-clockwise: the extreme northern tip of Scandinavia, including Biornøya Island, Jan Mayen Island and the Svalbard Islands, the northernmost edge of European Russia, with Franz Joseph Land, Kolguyev Island, Novaya Zemlya and Vaigach Island, and the northernmost edge of Asiatic Russia with the Severnaya Zemlya Islands, the New Siberia Islands, Wrangel Island and the Chukchi Peninsula.

Beyond the Bering Strait, the northern and northwestern coasts of Alaska are part of the Arctic, with the Pribilof, Nunivak, Saint Matthew, Saint Lawrence and Diomede Islands. The northern coast of Canada follows, with the great Canadian archipelago, Hudson Bay, except for the southern tip, all of Greenland, and the northern part of Iceland.

In northern Europe, the Gulf Stream brings warmth to Greenland, Iceland and as far up as the Svalbard Islands, sweeping along the coast of Scandinavia and making the climate less harsh. Its influence is so strong that Norway's climate remains sub-arctic up to the 71° parallel, while eastern Canada, bathed by the cold Labrador current, has a sub-arctic climate as far down as the 55° parallel.

In Europe, only the northern coasts of Norway and Russia have an Arctic climate. Scandinavia has a limited tundra area, with forests extending far north beyond the Gulf of Botnia.

The Kola Peninsula is flat and marshy, similar to the other coasts of European Russia, where the tundra area nevertheless widens, remaining broad until the Ural Mountains.

The influence of the Gulf Stream can be felt as far as Kolguyev Island and the western coast of Novaya Zemlya.

90 top left Lofoten Islands are mainly made of granitic mountains, cut almost vertically and modeled by winds and Quaternary glaciers. These rocky formations are to be considered among the oldest on the planet, according to some geologists.

90 top right In a fjord near Lingvaer, internal waters in the archipelago are tranquil. This body of water reflecting the mountains offers a breath-taking show, even more beautiful for the presence of winter ice.

90-91 When the weather is good, the Lofoten Islands offer enchanting, deserted landscapes like the one shown here of a fjord near the village of Smorten. In the winter a relatively stable high pressure system over northern Scandinavia protects the northern territories from extremely bad weather. Here the climate is less rigid than one might expect, due to the Gulf Stream. Temperatures drop below zero, nevertheless it is 15°-20° warmer than other places at the same latitude.

92 top The photo shows Knaevangen Fjord in the winter. The fjord is located in northern Norway, but the warm Gulf Stream permits trees to grow even at this latitude.

92-93 Arctic tundra greatly dominates the landscape of Finnmark. Only in well-protected areas birches and Arctic willows replace the tundra. The tundra in northern Europe extends from several hundred yards to several dozen miles from the seacoast.

93 top left In Finnmark, the interior of Norway inhabited mostly by the Saami, wonderful landscapes can be found. Dwellings are usually built close to trees protecting them from the north winds.

93 top right Finland is second only to European Russia in its number of lakes. In the far northern area, known as Lappi in Finnish, the thaw creates an intricate system of lakes, ponds and narrow strips of land between one body of water and another, which are impossible to cross without a local guide.

The sea, which keeps the Kola Peninsula free of ice, with the important port of Murmansk accessible all year round, only freezes partially toward the east.

As a consequence, even inland the climate is fairly mild, permitting birches and willows to take root quite far north.

Here the soil is a soft carpet of mosses and lichens, and even the herbaceous plants grow luxuriantly, providing enough forage to raise sheep and cows in addition to the ever-present reindeer. Biornøya Island (the island of bears) is part of Europe and is located halfway between Norway and the Svalbards.

It has a surface area of about 70 square miles and is geologically similar to the Svalbards.

The island has a vein of coal which was mined until the 1920's and later abandoned. The climate is harsh: the highest recorded temperature is 16° C, and there are only 7 clear days a year.

The climate is even harsher on Jan Mayen Island, immersed in its maritime polar climate about 300 miles from Greenland, about 400 miles from Iceland and nearly 600 from the Svalbards. It is the most isolated of the Arctic islands, with 15° C its highest recorded temperature and cloudy skies 8/10 of the year. It is 140 square miles in size and is almost completely covered by the extinct Beerenberg volcano, 7,500 feet high, covered with a great glacier, while other smaller glaciers flow down into the sea.

The Svalbard archipelago consists of two main islands, Vestspitsbergen (over 15,000 square miles in size) and Nordauslandet (about 6,000 square miles in size), as well as a group of smaller islands which includes Edgeöya, Barentsöya, Prins Karls Forland, Kong Karls Land, and Kwitöya, with a total surface area of a little less than 4,000 square miles.

The Svalbards, which were completely covered with ice in the Pleistocene age, still have numerous alpine-type glaciers, and deep fjords and glacial valleys furrow the larger islands.

The soil, most of which is barren, is covered with enough mosses and lichens to feed reindeer and musk oxen, the remains of much larger herds which were decimated by the fur trappers, who were once common on the islands. Arctic foxes

94 top Hall Island is in the southern part of Franz Josef Land and is part of the Russian Arctic, until very recently off-bounds to Westerners. The islands are separated by a maze of straits and channels, which are often impossible to navigate even in summer.

94-95 On the plateau of Kuhn Island a glacier carved its way slowly down to the sea.

95 top Cape Tagetthoff, taken from the name of the ship that sank here after the two Austrian explorers Payer and Weyprecht discovered the archipelago, is a superb monument of basalt rocks rising up on the coast, making it possible to identify Hall Island even from a distance.

95 bottom On nearly all the islands of the archipelago the glaciers flow down to reach the Arctic Ocean waters.

*96 top Another beautiful
image of Cape Tagetthoff
taken from land. Along
with Cape Flora on
Northbrook Island, it is a
landmark in the history
of Arctic exploration.
Famous explorers like
Nansen, Jackson, Ziegler*

*and Fiala all stopped
here. At Cape Flora one
can still clearly see the
stone plaque
commemorating the
deaths of three members
of the Duke of Abruzzi
expedition: Querini,
Ollier and Støkken.*

and hares are still common, as are lemmings, the preferred prey of the hundreds of thousands of migrating birds who nest on the coast.

Vestspitsbergen Island contains coal deposits which are mined by Norway and Russia at present. The Kong Karl Islands, which are less well-known than the others, have recently been transformed into a natural reserve for polar bears. Franz Joseph Land consists of a dozen islands and numerous islets, almost completely covered with glaciers.

The islands are almost exclusively basalt, and their present position seems to be the result of the break-up of an earlier large basalt plateau during the Pleistocene age, with deep channels developing between the current formations.

The archipelago lies in the pack-ice all year round, so that even navigating from one island to another is always quite risky. Polar bears and Arctic foxes live on the islands, along with great numbers of migrating birds. Many seals and walruses live in the sea.

This Russian archipelago still has weather and military stations which are accessible by ice breakers. The northernmost station is located on Prince Rudolph Island, the same area from which Cagni, the Italian explorer, departed during the 1899-1900 expedition to the North Pole, led by the Duke of Abruzzi.

There is another station on little Hayes Island, and finally a military station on Graham Bell Island, the easternmost island of the archipelago. Kolguyev Island, inhabited by fishermen, is a formation of sedimentary rock located near the delta of the Pechora River.

The island is one of the favorite nesting places of Asiatic species of wild swans, geese and ducks.

Vaigach Island and Novaya Zemlya may be considered the northern extension of the Urals, having the same geological structure. Vaigach Island is joined to the mainland in winter by an arm of ice, so the North-East route must run farther north through the Kara Strait. Novaya Zemlya consists of two islands.

The entire territory can be divided into three parts: the southernmost part up to 72° consists of a marshy lowland which is inhabited and fertile on the west coast, making it possible to breed reindeer, whereas the uninhabited east coast has a very harsh climate.

*96-97 This image shows
the hostility of the polar
climate at the latitudes
of Franz Josef Land, even
in the middle of summer.
Even before the
southernmost islands
come into sight, compact
pack-ice blocks access to
the north.*

*97 top Champ Island is
seen here from Cook
Channel. The island is
almost totally covered
with ice, has no accessible
points and played little
part in the history of past
explorations.*

*97 bottom A view of
Cape Germany on
Rudolph Island, the
northernmost island of
the entire archipelago.
The expedition on the
pack-ice organized by the
Duke of Abruzzi started
out from Tepliz Bay on
this island. Three sleds
took off, commanded by
Cagni, an Italian who
reached the highest
latitude ever, 86° 34' 49",
beating Nansen's previous
record of 86° 13'.*

100 top The Yakut
Republic covers the most
extensive territory of the
entire Union of Russian
Republics. The Lena
River runs south to north
across the territory. The
capital of Yakutsk is
located on the river, which
divides the territory
nearly in half. Yakut has
the lowest temperatures in
Siberia, down to 60°-70°
below zero. This picture
shows the unusual
appearance of the upper
course of the Siyaya River,
a tributary of the Lena,
which flows west of the
capital of Yakutsk.

100 center The Lena
River is frozen for eight
months a year and is
navigable from Yakutsk to
its mouth.

100 bottom left This
picture shows the flow of a
river in the Arctic coastal
area. In Yakut Republic
the timberline reaches
latitudes that elsewhere
are occupied by tundra.

101 After flowing briefly
through the hill region,
the Siyaya River runs
through the flatlands
covered with evergreen
forests.

102-103 The Kamchatka Peninsula extends north to south to the Pacific Ocean, breaking off from the Chukchi Peninsula. To the north, it is inhabited by the Koryaks, while the central and southern areas are home to the Itelmeni and the Nentsky. Not only is the land mountainous, but most of it is of volcanic origin. There are 29 active volcanoes, which offer a unique spectacle. There are over 40 inactive volcanoes, and over 50 percent of the land is covered with lava and ash. Volcanic activity extends to the northernmost areas of the Kurile Islands. In addition to volcanoes, the peninsula is full of geysers, calderas of boiling mud, hot underground rivers and solfataras. The typical sub-arctic vegetation is luxuriant, due to the very fertile soil. All photos were taken in the Kronotsky Wildlife Preserve in the east-central part of the peninsula.

*104-105 Kronotsky
Wildlife Preserve is full
of wild, pristine
landscape. The preserve is
also home to brown bears,
Arctic foxes, fur seals
and many species of
marine birds, as well as
eagles. Hundreds of
waterways flow down
from the central
mountain ranges and
empty primarily on the
west coast in the Sea of
Okhotsk. Kamchatka is
at the same latitude as
southern Alaska, on the
opposite side of the Pacific
Ocean. Both regions have
heavy rainfall and
persistent fog along the
coasts. The interior is
drier, as the numerous
mountains along the
eastern coast are a
barrier against the moist
winds of the Pacific.*

*106-107 A detail of the
vegetation on the
Kamchatka Peninsula in
Arctic Russia. The
flatland is entirely
covered by clusters of
bearberries, tufts of
tussock, a leathery plant
that forms pillows 12
inches high, sedges and
dwarf shrubs.*

108-109 The pack-ice moves away from the Alaska's coast late in the spring, breaking into millions of small and large fragments. The land ice, which is the first to form in the autumn and the last to melt in the summer, still clings to the coast.

less elevated. Numerous icebergs break off from both islands and remain trapped in the pack-ice drifting from east to west. Coming back to the continent, after the mouth of the Katanga, where the important city of Nordvik lies, the coast is precipitous until the delta of the Lena, with heights of up to 400 feet.

Beyond the great delta of this river, the coasts and tundra become lower, and the terrain consists of more or less agglomerate sands from the Pleistocene age. Cape Svatoi, which is formed of basalt and granite and is about 1,500 feet above sea level, stands out in this area. Laptev Strait separates Cape Svatoi from the islands of New Siberia, which consist of three large islands plus several smaller islands.

110-111 An iceberg, which still contains traces of moraine, floats in an inland lake in Iceland.

The southernmost one, Bolshoi Lyakowsky, is inhabited and is about 1,000 feet above sea level. The northernmost one, Kotelnyi, is the largest and most populous, with hills reaching almost 900 feet above sea level. The easternmost island is Novaya Sibir and gives its name to the archipelago. It is flat and uninhabited.

This group of islands is interesting because it has provided an incredible number of fossil mammoth tusks, most of which were sold to China. Records kept during the time of Czarist Russia show that as many as 22,000 tusks were sold between 1720 and 1730.

Proceeding along the continental coast, after Cape Svatoi, the land becomes flat and marshy up to the mouth of the Kolyma River, where a mountainous area begins that stretches to the Bering Strait, where Cape Dezhnev rises up almost 3,000 feet above sea level - a true Rock of Gibraltar in the Pacific.

The coast remains high and rugged to the mouth of the Anadyr River, which flows into the Pacific. Off the coast of the Chukchi Peninsula is the large island of Wrangel, with three villages inhabited by fishermen and hunters. The island's highest point is almost 3,000 feet, and walruses and seals are common in its waters.

Crossing the Bering Strait, we find the large Alaskan Peninsula, the westernmost edge of the North American continent. Only about 150,000 square miles, or one quarter of its total surface area, can be considered Arctic. This would include in particular the northern coast with its tundra, and the western coast to the mouth of the Kuskokwim River.

Polar Alaska can be divided into four areas: 1) the northern region, which includes the vast, flat, marshy region north of the Brooks Range; 2) the Seward Peninsula; 3) the lowlands which include the deltas of the Yukon and Kuskokwim rivers; 4) the islands close to the Bering Strait.

The northern region includes the Brooks Range, whose tallest peak is Doonerak at almost 9,000 feet. A broad terrace 93 miles long and 2,600 feet high runs between the mountain range and the sea, while the remaining territory is a marshy lowland that stretches to the coast, which is full of lagoons. Along the coast are important towns such as Barrow, Alaska's northernmost city, Prudhoe Bay and Kaktovik. The second zone begins with the Seward Peninsula.

Along with the Chukchi Peninsula lying on the opposite side, it divides the Chuckchi Sea from the Bering Sea and is the westernmost part of the United States, at Cape Prince of Wales. There are two islands off this cape: Big Diomede, which belongs to Russia, and Little Diomede, which is American.

The international date line runs between the two islands: for example, when it is midnight on Sunday at Little Diomede, it is midnight on Monday at Big Diomede.

The most important city on the peninsula is Nome, famous for having been the center of the Gold Rush in 1899, when large quantities of gold were found on the coast.

The Iditarod Race, the longest dogsled race in the world, is still held here.

It runs one thousand miles on a rough course that starts at Anchorage and ends at Nome.

The third zone begins south of Norton Gulf. This region includes the mouths of the Yukon and Kuskokwim Rivers and is essentially flat, with a myriad of lagoons, ponds and lakes.

The land is so flat that the tides rise up in the two rivers for as far as 30-35 miles.

The two most important towns are Saint Michael and Bethel at the mouth of the Kuskokwim. The fourth region includes Saint Lawrence Island, the largest and the oldest of the islands in the area, with rocks dating back to the Paleozoic epoch. It is also important for archaeological finds, almost all of which are ivory objects and figurines which come from the Bering Eskimo culture and date from about 2000 BC. Nunivak Island is the cone of an extinct volcano almost 2,000 feet high; its vegetation, consisting of mosses and lichens, makes it possible to breed reindeer and musk oxen here, which were introduced to the island by Norway and Canada.

Remote Saint Matthew Island and the Pribilof Islands are also of volcanic origin and have a rather rich tundra vegetation.

The most important are the Pribilof Islands, which are famous for their approximately 2 million fur seals, hunted for their valuable furs. After the islands were first discovered in 1786, the fur seals were hunted to the verge of extinction by both the Russians and the Americans. Since 1911 hunting has been strictly regulated, and now there are once again 2 million fur seals, probably the maximum the waters can support.

As a result of the regulation, 70,000 three-years old males are caught each year, without decreasing the total number of fur seals.

Lying next to Alaska, the Canadian Arctic includes the mountainous Yukon territory with its important city of Whitehorse, which is on the Alaska Highway that connects British Columbia with Point Barrow.

112 and 113 top The disintegrating pack-ice photographed at Beechey Island across from large Devon Island in the Canadian archipelago.

112-113 This photo shows the odd geometrical effects produced by the pack-ice off the coast of Somerset Island in the Canadian archipelago at the end of Lancaster Strait.

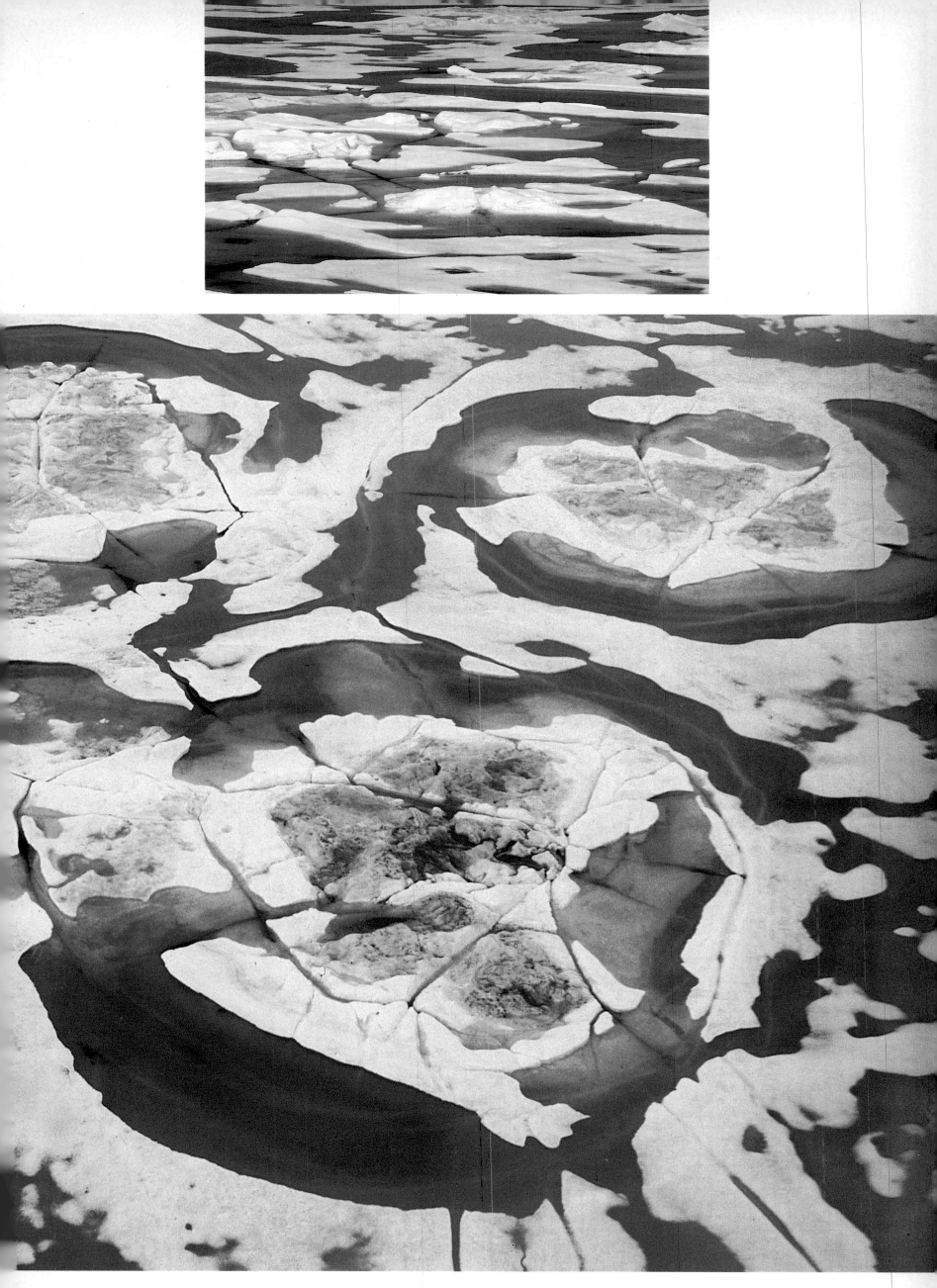

Islands, and has the same rocks from the ancient Canadian shield that originated during the Paleozoic epoch, covered with fragments of volcanic rock from the Tertiary Age. There are other interesting facts about Greenland. For one thing, its structure is an immense basin with edges consisting of rocky formations which contain the great glacial mass.

All of its mountains, with the possible exception of those buried beneath the layer of ice, are at the edge of the land with those on the eastern coast being much higher than those on the western coast.

The four tallest peaks are Gunnbjørns Field, at 12,000 feet, Forel Bjerg at over 11,000 feet, Perfektnunatak at almost 10,000 feet, and Petermann Bjerg at 9,700 feet. Even the inland ice is not symmetrical at the east and west coasts; if we look at a section at any latitude, we will see that the ice cap reaches its maximum height and maximum thickness in the eastern part, while it decreases both to the west and to the north.

The reason for this asymmetry is the greater precipitation in the east, while the elevation of the underlying earth is of no consequence.

It is at a constant 700-1,700 feet below sea level in the central portion, rising gradually near the coasts. A singular feature, which is also present in the Antarctic, is the mountain peaks poking out of the ice cover at the edge of the inland ice.

These peaks are known to the Eskimos as nunataks, a term which is now also used in the Alps and Himalayas.

The numerous finds of fossil plants indicate that Greenland's climate was mild or even warm during the Tertiary epoch, until a series of glaciations in the Quaternary gradually covered the island with the thick coat of ice that persists even today, although it is very slowly retreating.

Geoseismic and gravimetric surveys performed on the inland ice have revealed that Greenland is crossed by two large fractures at the 69° and 71° parallel, running from coast to coast.

This means that the great island is actually three smaller islands welded together by the glacial mass. Unlike other Arctic territories, in Greenland there is no transition from taiga to tundra, even though about one quarter of the land is below the Arctic Circle.

The ice-free coastal areas are gathered on the western side between the 61° and 73° parallel and on the eastern side between the 70° and 78° parallel, and a vast area in the north up to the spit of land closest to the pole at 83° 40' is also ice-free. An examination of the land shows that it was never covered by previous glaciations.

The southern area, which is rainier and has a less stable climate than the rest of the island, is suitable for raising sheep and cattle.

Elsewhere, the ice-free area is covered with mosses and lichens, and many small flowering plants can be seen on land which was the result of an eruption. Reforesting with trees adapted to the Arctic climate has been attempted in southern Greenland, with birches so far producing the best results. With respect to vegetation, a curious anomaly should be noted: on the northeast coast, swept by the frigid glacial current that descends down to the 74° parallel, where a perennial ice-pack makes all access to the sea impossible, the flora is more varied, with more species than in the rest of the island.

Naturalists have dubbed this coast the Arctic Riviera, and little flowering plants appear even in the far north, along with numerous insects and four species of butterfly.

Finally, we come to the inland ice. Visible from many points on the coast, it is a spectacular phenomenon that always fascinates visitors to this truly singular island. The Eskimos, or more accurately the Greenlanders, have for centuries viewed the inland ice with terror and have carefully avoided it, calling it the "great ice monster." This monster's tentacles are the flowing tongues of ice that dump portions of the inland ice into the coastal sea.

Across the glacial valleys, taking the path of least resistance, fast-flowing peripheral glaciers (for example, the Jakobshaven glacier moves 100 feet a day), reach the water, float for a brief period and then break into the large blocks we know as icebergs, which drift with the winds and currents once they are dumped into the sea.

Only 1/5 to 1/9 of their total volume can be seen on the surface once the icebergs fall into the sea. This depends on the type of ice: older ice is heavier, while more recent ice still contains a certain amount of air.

124 Brodeur Peninsula is the westernmost part of large Baffin Island in the Canadian archipelago. In the foreground is Cape Van Koenig and Bernier Bay to the right, and the large tract of frozen sea is Prince Regent Bay.

124-125 Due to the combined effect of winds and currents, in the spring this portion of the sea is completely free of pack-ice.

125 top This is a typical view of the shattered ice-pack in late spring.

126 Spring has arrived, but on Baffin Island in the Canadian archipelago, winter ice still grips the northern part of the island. These images give a good idea of the size of the Arctic archipelago.

127 While the sea still shows signs of summer, with only a few remnants of fragmented pack-ice, in the interior the first snows of September have already blanketed the coast of the peninsula of Scoresby Sound, in eastern Greenland.

The Jakobshaven glacier, the most prolific glacier in Greenland, produces an amazing 25,000 tons of ice a day. Adding up the production of all glaciers that flow into the sea, we obtain the mind-boggling amount of 370 million tons.

Finally, we should recall that Greenland's coast is quite rugged, including thousands of fjords, almost all of which originated from glacial valleys.

The longest is Scoresby Sound on the east coast, which at 180 miles is the longest in the world. The most noteworthy fjords on the eastern coast are Nordre Strømfjord, 114 miles long, and Sondre Strømfjord, 100 miles.

The northern coast of Iceland, which is not affected by the Gulf Stream, has a partially Arctic climate. The island is about 40,000 square miles in size and is located about 160 miles from Greenland, 478 miles from Scotland and 600 miles from Norway. The land is for the most part barren, due to the presence of large glaciers and recent lava and ash from the eruption of numerous volcanoes which became extinct only recently. The largest glacier, Vatnajökull, is 7,300 square miles in size and rises up to an elevation of 7,000 feet.

Three other large glaciers, all in the south central part of the island, are together as large as the ones mentioned above. Glaciers cover a total of 1/8 of the island's entire surface.

There are nearly no trees on Iceland, which can be divided into two climate zones. The northern zone, with little precipitation, is covered with tundra, with a few herbaceous plants and dwarf shrubs, whereas the southern zone is rather rainy and provides rich forage for animals, mostly sheep. The largest waterfalls in Europe are in Iceland, and there are also numerous geysers, violent jets of hot water and steam which erupt intermittently from the earth.

Another feature of this island is the eruption of large quantities of volcanic lava from the sea near the coast. As this lava cools, it forms little islets, and as soon as they are cool enough marine birds from the upper Arctic promptly begin using them for nesting. In fact, many species prefer to pass the winter in Iceland rather than on the closer continent. In summer, millions of birds, primarily geese, ducks and waders, make their nests in Iceland.

128-129 The Kangerdlugssuaq glacier with its large basin is located north of the Wegener Peninsula in northwest Greenland. Despite the wide river of ice that starts within the inland ice and flows into the sea, this is one of the least prolific glaciers in Greenland in terms of producing icebergs. Note how the ice flow, which here joins two branches coming from different directions, does not carry a trace of medial moraine, making it an anomaly. It flows on a gentle slope almost to the sea, where the formation of crevasses crossing this flow signals a further decrease in the incline.

130-131 This winter photo shows sea ice and the rocky coasts plunging into Lancaster Sound. During the summer, this strait in the Canadian archipelago is ice-free and constitutes the first leg of the Northwest Passage, starting from Baffin Bay.

132 top Two old women from the Coppermine Inuit dance to the rhythmic beat of a drum played by another woman, while younger people look on.

132-133 Young Jamiesie Mucktar, an Inuk from Baffin Island in the Canadian archipelago, was photographed at Pond Inlet, a village on the northern coast of the island.

MAN AND ICE: FOR THOUSANDS OF YEARS, A STORY OF DAILY HEROISM

133 A popular game among the Inuit of northern Alaska, one of the few indigenous peoples who still hunt whales, is bouncing on a cloth held taut by a group of friends. Walrus skins sewn into a circular form were once used in this ancient tradition.

Small groups of peoples have lived around the Arctic inland sea for millennia. Their language and racial origins are different, but they are united by a great similarity in material culture. This culture has permitted Arctic tribes to survive and overcome the terrible environmental conditions, both on the half-frozen ocean coasts and in the tundra.

This primitive culture, at first unappreciated, was finally understood and assimilated by those who had to adopt the lifestyle of local populations if they wanted to continue their activities in these latitudes.

It was only by using their means of transport, a sled pulled by polar dogs, and their clothing, consisting of layers of fur, that the explorers Peary (1909) and Amundsen (1911) reached the North Pole and the South Pole respectively, successfully completing their difficult routes. Another explorer, Stefansson, crossed northern Canada without an expedition, counting only on the help of a companion and two rifles, thus demonstrating that barren areas seemingly void of life could offer humans adequate means for survival.

The Eskimos are the most thoroughly studied Arctic population and the group which has best adapted to the difficult Arctic living conditions. The term Eskimo comes from the Cree dialect of the Algonquin Indians, who disdainfully referred to them as "eaters of raw meat." Today the Eskimos occupy only a very tiny territory on the easternmost tip of Asia.

In the distant past they traveled across the Bering Strait (which at that time was probably still a spit of land that joined the two continents) and settled throughout North America from Alaska to Greenland. But there are other peoples in the Eurasian Arctic who lead a very similar lifestyle.

All of these peoples have always been distinguished by several basic elements: fishing, hunting of sea animals, breeding of reindeer and traveling by dogsled.

The first activity is almost universal, the second and the third may be alternative, and the last is a specialization practiced only by certain peoples. If we cross the entire Arctic in a counter clockwise direction, taking Lapland

as West and Greenland as East, we can draw a curve to show where reindeer are raised by tracing the highest point West, then descending to the lowest East. After the Bering Strait, the dog becomes the familiar element in Eskimo culture. The Eskimos live in true symbiosis with this animal as it is an indispensable part of their lifestyle. In the case of dog breeding, a line can be traced that starts from zero at the point indicated as West and reaches its apex once it passes the Bering Strait. The only exception to the perfect mirror image of the two lines is the overlap at Chukchi, where the coastal populations are

hunters who use dogs and sleds, while the inland inhabitants are reindeer herders.

The division of Arctic peoples in Eurasia is quite complex, as various populations overlap in the same territory, and settlements never have a unitary organization that would classify them as nations. Moreover, some populations have settled in various areas of the Arctic.

Within a few miles there will be inhabitants who do not even understand their neighbors' language. This century-old isolation made it impossible for these peoples to push back invaders, the first of whom were Russians, who conquered the whole Siberian territory between 1583 and 1642 when they reached the coast of the Pacific Ocean. The courageous Chukchi

134 In the Russian sub-arctic, two Nentsky were photographed with their sled on Kanin Peninsula in European Russia. The Nentsky are semi-nomadic reindeer breeders with customs quite similar to the Saami or Lapps.

135 Noah, a Caribou Inuk from the Baker Lake region in central Canada, stands next to his tent made of caribou hides stitched together and stretched out on wooden poles. Note the simple but refined elegance of his clothing, all of which, including the boots, is made of extremely soft caribou hide.

with their dedication to the land were the last people to resist Russia's domination.

They defended their land inch by inch, avoiding direct encounters through their extraordinary mobility due to the skillful use of dogs and sleds. Despite the brutal oppression and exploitation of the native people, the Russians did provide at least some benefit for such heterogeneous populations: the Russian language was gradually adopted by everyone so that the new Russians could understand each other through a common language, just as English gave India a means of unifying different ethnic groups that spoke a thousand different dialects.

We should also mention another historic fact which books often ignore: even in the 17th century Siberia was a land of prisons and political exile, and those deported to the eastern territories often outnumbered the local population.

Many of them escaped, disappearing into unexplored territory, sometimes finding refuge with the local people.

Certainly there were thousands of cases of interbreeding with natives, a fact which has recently been noted in studies which came to light in the post-Soviet era.

The inhabitants of Siberia can be divided into five principal groups, which in keeping with convention will be indicated as "races":

1) the Lapps or Samek;
2) the Finno-Ugric peoples;
3) the Tungus-Manchu peoples;
4) the Turki-Yakuts;
5) the Paleoasians.

It has been established that groups 3 and 4 were the most recent invaders of the Arctic, while groups 2 and 5 (Eskimos are part of the latter) are the oldest inhabitants.

The Lapps, who also speak a Finno-Ugric language, but in a completely different way, having lost the agglutinated character typical of these languages, are a mystery unto themselves. Although they have settled within the countries of Norway, Sweden and Finland (only a small group lives on the Kola Peninsula under Russian authority), the Lapps have maintained an admirable cultural unity that they cultivate passionately. Today their lives are less harsh

The Sami people or Lapps live in tribes in the Arctic regions of Sweden, Finland and Russia, as well as Norway, and they are the real lords of the great empty spaces of the far north. They have always been nomads, dependent on reindeer which, until a few years ago, were their staple and their fortune. Now the Sami have their own representatives in parliament, their own radio stations, newspapers and magazines (the Sami language belongs to a totally different group from the other Scandinavian languages). The traditional dress of Sami men is a heavy blue tunic richly finished with red bands and colored ribbons, drawn in at the waist with a belt and worn over reindeer-leather trousers; the women's costume is longer and flared, with a fringed shawl to add a feminine touch. While all Sami have much the same footwear, their hats - and especially the ones worn by men - change in style from tribe to tribe.

than in the past, but are still affected by the polar climate and the dangers of such a vast, semi-desert area.

This may be why, when they are not busy struggling against great distances and the elements, the Lapps try to make every spare moment an occasion for fun and socializing.

The spring meetings during the Easter festivities are well known, when entire families set out to bring finished products to market and buy raw materials and equipment.

Groups which have been separated for years meet and celebrate during the event. It is also a good time to celebrate marriages and settle financial matters.

During these meetings, there are also athletic contests and games of skill, such as a dangerous race on skis pulled by specially trained reindeer.

The Finno-Ugric peoples are today represented by the Nentsky, who live from the Kola Peninsula to the Jamal Peninsula. Like the Lapps, they are primarily reindeer herders and use the reindeer as a means of transport. The Komi, who live west of the Urals, are part of the same racial group, while the Voguls and Ostiaks live east of this mountain range, far from the Arctic coast. Farther east live the Samoyed on the cold Taimyr Peninsula.

Farther inland are the Evenki, of Tungus-Manchu stock, while the Evenian and the Yakuts, who speak a Turkic language, have settled in the wide area including the basins of the rivers Lena and Indigirca, as well as in the eastern portion of the central Siberian plateau. To the east of Yakutsk are Paleoasian peoples, including the Yukagiri, the Chukchi, the Koriaks, and the Itelmeni mixed with the Nentsky, a Finno-Ugric population.

Eurasians occupy the great Chukchi Peninsula, except for a tongue of land settled by about one thousand Asiatic Eskimos, and the Kamchatka Peninsula and the northern part of Sakhalin Island, where the Ghiliaks live.

The vast territory that faces the Okhost Sea is inhabited by Evenians and Evenki, both of whom are of Tungus-Manchu origin. As can be seen, there is no large area of Siberia without multiple ethnic groups overlapping each other.

138 Note the elegant costume of this well-to-do Sami reindeer breeder, with its prevalence of traditional blues and reds. His cylindrical hat is decorated with colorful ribbons and his jacket is fastened with a silver buckle. Other items of jewelry can be seen around the shirt collar. The photo was taken in Kautokeinom in Norwegian Lapland.

139 top A breeder in the middle of his herd of reindeer, during the winter sojourn in the forested area of Norwegian Lapland.

139 bottom A Sami woman assigned to reindeer breeding has collected an antler shed by a reindeer during the winter gathering.

140 top and 140-141 This photo shows preparations for the reindeer race at Kautokeinom in Finnmark. The event draws a great number of Sami or Lapps, from neighboring communities in Sweden and Finland as well. Recently the spring games, which coincide with Easter festivities, have attracted large numbers of tourists from all over the world.

141 top This Sami girl was photographed in Kautokeinom. As can be seen, there is a great variety of facial features among the Sami; some have Mongoloid features, while others appear European and are almost indistinguishable from Scandinavians.

141 center This photo shows part of the reindeer race; in this case the competitor guides the reindeer from a sled. The reindeer's antlers have not been cruelly sawed from its head, but have been shed naturally for the winter and will grow back again in the spring.

141 bottom This reindeer-skin boot, with only the toe tied to the ski, makes it possible to move by pushing into the snow. It is used mainly in Finnish Lapland, but can also be found throughout Lapland, with slight variations.

142 top An aerial photograph of Hetta in Finnish Lapland. Lakes and rivers are erased by the ice and snow, spattered with dark expanses of red fir forests.

142 center Here is a service station in Finnmark. The Sami find snowmobiles quite useful for following and herding reindeer.

142 bottom A young Sami woman appears in her traditional dress in a Hetta supermarket.

142-143 A Sami woman in her home in Finland uses a small loom to produce traditional designs to decorate clothing.

143 top A bride and groom photographed after a wedding ceremony celebrated in the Lutheran church in Kautokeinom in Finnmark. The typical silver-plated ornaments, particularly rich on this occasion, are handed down from generation to generation.

144-145 Reine is in the Lofoten Islands of Norway. The village is on the southern tip of Flakstad Island. A few miles south of Reine, the waters of the sea churn, moved by the northern Atlantic current which encounters the Lofoten Islands and turns back on itself. This is the famous Maelstrom, the terror of endless generations of sailors.

146 top A group of Caribou Inuit moves in the evening light near Baker Lake, in the Canadian Barren Lands not far from Hudson Bay.

146-147 *Two Inuits are seen in the evening light before their caribou hide tent. Note the clothing with the fur turned inward as well as their unique glasses, made of a strip of wood with two slits carved into it, permitting them to see without being blinded by the light.*

147 top *Noah plays with a small hollow bone tied with a leather lace. This diversion consists of using a flip of the wrist to toss the cylinder of bone into a holder held in the hand.*

147 bottom *In this traditional dance Noah moves to the rhythm of a drum made of caribou hide pulled taut over a circular frame.*

The situation is certainly simpler on the other side of the Bering Strait. First of all, there are only two populations, the Aleutians and the Eskimos. The former occupies the long arc of islands that edges the Bering Sea and also live on the Russian island of Komandorskie off the coast of Kamchatka. The Eskimo population is scattered along a coastal area 5,500 miles long that runs from the Bering Strait to eastern Greenland and are therefore divided into many small groups.

Near the strait live the so-called Strait Eskimos. Farther north, up to the Canadian border, live the Eskimos of northern Alaska. Below the flow of the river Yukon live the Eskimos of western Alaska, while the Chugach Eskimos live along the Gulf of Alaska. The Mackenzie Eskimos live in Canada. The Copper Eskimos live on Victoria Island and on the mainland across from it. The Caribou Eskimos live on the Keewatin Peninsula, while the Labrador Eskimos live on the Ungava Peninsula and in Labrador. The Netsilik Eskimos live on the eastern coast of the Keewatin Peninsula; the Igloolik Eskimos and the Baffin Eskimos live on Baffin Island. Finally, the Southampton Eskimos live on Southampton Island in the northern part of Hudson Bay. The Polar Eskimos live in Greenland in the northernmost permanent settlement in the Arctic. There are also the Eskimos of the west coast, which is more populous, and those of the east coast, which is more sparsely populated.

Although there are some differences, Eskimo racial characteristics are easy to describe. The people are small, with short legs and arms, and a very robust trunk. Their hands and feet are also small. The head is big and elongated. The face is long and broad with a thin short nose, high cheekbones and particularly developed chewing muscles. Their skin is yellowish, their eyes usually very dark and the Mongolic ocular fold is common. The hair on their heads is straight and black, and they have little other body hair. These factors including the short limbs, which require less work for the heart to keep the extremities warm, and the narrow nasal passage, which makes it easier to heat the air that reaches the lungs, are considered

adaptations to the polar climate. In addition, Eskimos are known for their ability to digest and assimilate greater quantities of fats than any other race.

The material culture of the Eskimos, who call themselves the Inuit, which means "human beings", coincides with the ingenious use of the extremely few materials they have available. The Arctic is notoriously lacking in timber, except for the small amounts carried in by the currents. The only workable metal, copper, is found exclusively in the central part of the Canadian Arctic and was little used because the melting process was unknown. Steatite, or soapstone, which is easy to work, was instead used to build kudliks, an oil lamp that burned whale fat or other animal fats and both illuminated and

heated the dwelling. The wick was made from dried moss, and it was commonly held that a worthy woman kept the lamp lit all through the night, keeping the home constantly warm.

Two Eskimo words, kayak and igloo (from the Inuit word iglu), have become universally popular. The kayak, an extremely light boat consisting of a light framework covered with shaved seal fur, is one of the most refined examples of Eskimo culture. Kayak building skills reach their height in Greenland. Aided by an ingenious invention, the harpoon with a bone tip, Eskimos do not hesitate to face large prey, including whales, with an amazing combination of dexterity, mobility and courage.

The classic igloo, built of blocks of snow cut with a special knife, is a true piece of skilled architecture that combines resistance against weather, insulation and speed of construction. An expert can build a basic igloo structure in less than an hour, subsequently filling the cracks with pressed snow in less than a half hour. Inside, the temperature may be 40°-50° warmer than the outside. The entrance, consisting of a tunnel made of snow blocks and facing away from the wind, is a comfortable shelter for the dogs. An igloo can be built in various sizes, depending on whether it is used as a temporary shelter during a hunting trip or as a dwelling to house the whole family for an extended period of time. Igloo-making is not common to the entire Arctic: it has always been unknown in Greenland and Alaska, where tents built with poles and animal skins functioned as temporary structures.

A more permanent dwelling is dug into the earth and its roof is made of skins stretched out on whale ribs, birch branches, or driftwood washed up on the beach. Peat can also be used to reinforce the walls and protect the construction from the cold winter winds. These types of dwelling allow the inhabitants to stand upright inside.

In the past, Eskimo clothing consisted of skins, including caribou, seal or Polar-bear skins. In Greenland, polar bear skins were used only for male trousers. Caribou hide was worn with the fur side touching the body, and other skins were used for beds and, during the coldest months, as inside tent coverings. An extremely

148 In the Canadian Arctic, in the Baker Lake area, Elizabeth, an Inuit woman from the Caribou population, carries half a caribou carcass on her shoulders after having skinned the animal.

149 A close-up of Ruth, an old Inuit woman. Note her clothing with the fur side against the skin, her Indian braids and the elegantly decorated collar.

150-151 *The igloo is
nearly complete. This is
the most difficult part of
the construction, when
the blocks of snow are
placed nearly horizontally
to form the roof.*

151 top *The last blocks of
snow are taken from a
larger block placed
within the igloo.*

151 bottom *The Inuit
with their hoods pulled up
despite the sunny day give
an idea of how cold it is.
Under these conditions,
the snow becomes the
perfect consistency for
making an igloo.*

valuable part of the caribou was the tendons, which were used to make clothing and stitch together the skins used to cover kayaks and umiaks. Umiaks were roomy, open-hulled boats which were used to transport families and household goods. Caribou tendons, which expand upon contact with water, make the seams completely waterproof. Seal-skin was also widely used for outer jackets, trousers, and boots. Cut into narrow strips, it was used to make dog harnesses, sled straps and whips. The narrow strips were also knotted together to connect an entire seal-skin, sewn together and filled with air, to the tip of a harpoon to prevent captured prey from sinking.

Washed and dried seal intestines provided a translucent material used to build rudimentary windows, both in igloos and in peat structures. Bear-skin was also used to make soles of boots which were especially silent and non-slippery. Their insulating properties proved very useful during the hunters' long waits in the Polar cold. Bear-skin was also cut into thin strips used to cover sled runners. This very strong material could withstand jolts against fresh ice and would slide well on the soft snow. Wolf and wolverine skins were used to trim the hoods of parkas, outer jackets made of seal-skin. Even bird feathers were sewn together to make shirts to be worn against the skin.

Vegetation was scarcely used: dried moss was used for lamp wicks, and the resinous cassiope was used in the summer as fuel, and all year round by inland tribes with no access to animal oil. The only fruits available were blueberries, and these were eaten for an extra dose of vitamin C the needs for which was also met by the skin of the narwhal and by various animal organs, eaten either raw or barely heated.

With meat as the main if not only part of their diet, it is easy to see why hunting was absolutely vital to Eskimos. Seals, walruses, beluga whales and narwhals were hunted in the summer, from kayaks or on slabs of ice next to the shore. If a large whale was killed, it provided abundant food for the entire winter. Caribou were hunted with primitive weapons, including bows and arrows and lances, after a small group of animals was forced into a certain area, sometimes with the use of little stone men.

152 top An Inuk from the Caribou population makes a hole for ice fishing on Baker Lake.

152-153 Two Inuit from the Caribou population in the Baker Lake district, their hoods pulled up close to protect them from the intense cold, quickly eat a freshly-caught fish before it freezes.

153 top An old Inuit, also protected by heavy clothing, wears the spectacles made of wood that allow him to see without being blinded by the intense light reverberating on the snow.

Women were responsible for preparing the hides, and often chewed the hard material to make it soft and workable.

Freshwater fish were caught with arrows in the summer, while in the winter they were caught by making holes in the frozen surface and using a special harpoon. When the salmon were running, the Eskimos could accumulate large fish reserves, which they generally smoked or hid under piles of snow to protect them from foxes, dogs and bears. Eskimo children collected bird eggs, and birds were also hunted, especially guillemots, who would be caught in nets as they skimmed the surface in large flocks.

Eskimo populations have always had a philosophy of utilitarian nomadism, and they followed the best hunting grounds as the seasons changed. The migration of the caribou, the arrival of the birds, and the passage of the cetaceans were only a few of the important seasonal events the Eskimos followed.

Although the old social order has changed profoundly over the past century, in order to better understand the consequences of this people's meeting with Western culture, we should briefly outline their social organization over past centuries. The Eskimos were certainly part of one of those early Stone Age cultures which did not have any complex tribal structure. The family, or at the most a few families, constituted the largest organized unit. In some cases the group recognized a highly authoritative member, for example a good hunter whose skill and courage could influence the fate of the entire group.

If no such a person was present, a shaman would hold authority. Shamans were a common feature of not only Eskimo society, but of all Arctic peoples. The shaman represented the Eskimo's need to communicate with deities or spirits to ensure the success of a hunt or as a means to gain pardon for violating certain taboos. The shaman was also responsible for curing illnesses and preventing disasters which could affect the entire community. In other words, in the material poverty of the Eskimo world, the shaman represented a flight from the daily fears and misery of the people and offered a glimpse into a spiritual world which, although naive and primitive, nevertheless satisfied their

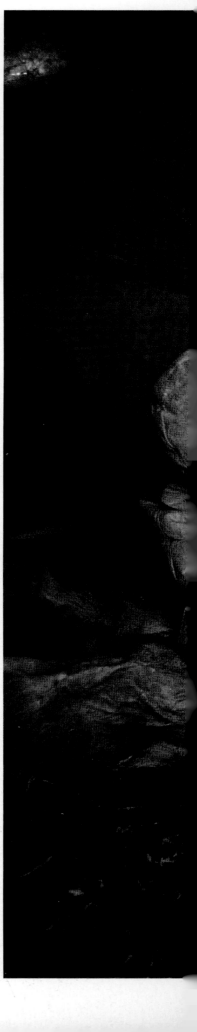

155 top The tent is finally set up. The two couples enjoy the heat produced by the traditional steatite lamp known as a kudlik, which is usually fed with seal or whale fat, but can also work with fish, bird and caribou fat.

needs. We should not, however, underestimate the fact that the Eskimos and their social organization were perfectly in harmony with the extraordinary environment around them. Even today, an Eskimo in the middle of a blizzard cutting blocks of snow for the foundation of an igloo may stop for a while as the darkness grows to smoke his pipe before continuing his work.

Primitive Eskimos had four important psychological attributes. The first was great esteem for their own personal ability, with the belief that they could provide for both themselves and their own families.

The second attribute was the fact that Eskimos placed little value on the personal possession of property. Because they were nomads, they owned only the few goods which could be transported by sled or boat. This resulted in an essential honesty: the Eskimos had no inclination to accumulate goods or assets for the future. These two attributes, their proud self-esteem and the low value placed on personal property, resulted in a great generosity and sincere pleasure in giving their belongings to others. They who could give things to others were worthy people, making it impossible for the person receiving not to esteem and admire them. The Eskimos showed equal disinterest for the lands and entire territory they occupied. The land had value only if it was used for a certain purpose, hunting or fishing.

The third great attribute was the group's solidarity as a means for survival in their harsh environment. It could be described as a primitive form of communism, in which the available food was divided equally among all members of the community. To protect the group in times of great hunger, female infanticide was practiced, while males were allowed to live because they would become good hunters. In addition, when elderly members of the group were no longer able to contribute to the community, thus becoming a burden for everyone, they committed suicide by exposure to intense cold. It should be noted that this did not occur without great suffering for those who were forced to assist them in such a terrible moment. A consequence of the second and third attributes was that the Eskimos were

neither jealous nor possessive of their consorts. Husbands and wives were exchanged without scandal. They were not overly possessive of their children either, although they took good care of them and loved them deeply. There was a large number of adoptions, to provide a balance between a family which was too large and another which wanted children. The Eskimo family was a natural family in the etymological sense, wary of any excessive authority. Everyone, even young people, had a responsible, respected position.

The fourth typical attribute of the Eskimos was the extreme passivity and patience shown in personal relationships, which allowed them to appear serene and impassive, even in the most critical situations. This permitted them to behave in a correct and determined way. Moreover, Eskimos never gave direct orders to their companions or others. Rather than a clear order: "Close the door!" they might say, "Doesn't it seem drafty near the door?", or instead of "Set sail!" they would prefer to paraphrase it: "Shouldn't we raise anchor now?" A famous ethnologist wrote that if Western society is fated to erase Eskimo culture from the face of the Earth, the white man should at least try to emulate some of the Eskimos' lessons in personal relations before destroying them.

The first Eskimos and Aleutians came to North America across what is now the Bering Strait, about 8,000-10,000 years ago. They traveled by boat or they crossed over the isthmus joining Asia and America which had been formed during the last glaciation, called Würm, that lowered the sea level by over 400 feet. The strait area, including St. Lawrence Island, contains old vestiges dating back over 4,000 years ago which testify to the passage of people in those remote epochs. When the glaciation was over, the sea level rose again, allowing large cetaceans to enter the Arctic. The waters of the Bering Sea were settled by many pinnipeds, and caribou became abundant inland. Beyond doubt, an early culture formed near this bridgehead. In time, it broke into three branches: the Aleutians, with their own language, the Eskimos of southern Alaska, and the Strait Eskimos. Little is known of the course

158 top left In Melville Bay in northwest Greenland, a hunter surrounded by his sled dogs stands on the crest of a pressure dike to get a better look at a bear.

158 bottom left An Inuk in northwestern Greenland slakes his thirst from a puddle of freshwater formed during the summer thaw of an iceberg.

158-159 This was taken in the Canadian Arctic at Resolute Bay on Cornwallis Island. The Inuk hunter Simon Idlout surveys the pack ice in search of possible prey.

159 top An Inuk hunter proceeds on all fours on the ice-pack as he attempts to approach a seal. To camouflage himself, he uses a little wood frame covered with white cloth with a small hole in the middle.

this latter group followed in its march eastward to Greenland. The Arctic area on the American side of the Bering Strait to Greenland is 5,400 miles long, and the bone, wood and animal skin dwellings this people used have left no discernible traces over the millennia. A single important discovery has been made at Norton Sound; known as the Denbigh Flint Complex, it consists of artifacts from the Paleolithic and Mesolithic. Five thousand years of time separate this find from the one at Cape Dorset on the southern tip of Baffin Island. The primitive culture of this island did not use bows or dogsleds, nor did it hunt large cetaceans. From this we can deduce that this line broke off from the Bering Strait culture before it reached its apex. It was still present in eastern Canada when the more sophisticated Thule culture, which developed in northern Greenland, prevailed throughout the Arctic, dominating for almost a millennium until modern times.

The explorer Rasmussen first demonstrated this cultural unity, with its extraordinarily small population scattered over an extraordinarily large area. At the end of his famous Thule Expeditions from 1920-1930, Rasmussen discovered that the Eskimos of the Bering Strait could understand the language he spoke in Greenland. Thus, modern-day Eskimos are the direct descendants of the Thule people, and what little ancestral tradition still survives is due to the strong roots of a system of life so sound and natural to these people that it survived the lure of another civilization.

The above description of Eskimo life and culture refers to the period up to the Second World War. This people had already had two traumatic encounters with the whalers and the fur traders.

Contact with the new arrivals had had many negative consequences, including previously unknown diseases, alcoholism and exploitation in general, as highly valuable skins were traded for worthless objects.

Nevertheless, the life of the American Arctic, including Greenland, held true to its traditional culture, made up of sacrifice and risks, with a population scattered in small communities that were often inaccessible in

161 top left This old Inuk hunter's breath condensed on his beard as he drove his dog sled. Today, young Inuit prefer snowmobiles, but old hunters feel that a team of dogs gives them more autonomy and is more reliable. Moreover, when the fog rolls in unexpectedly, dogs can find their way home alone.

161 top right This Inuk after killing a bear is going to cut out the heart and drink the warm blood. The removal of the animal's heart is a ritual that continues to this day and is a remnant of the animistic religion the Inuit have practiced for millennia. As the heart is seen as the vital center of every creature by drinking its blood the hunter establishes a kinship with the victim and removes any anger directed at the hunter or his family. Apart from the heart, the choicest edible part is the tongue, whereas Polar bear liver is toxic to both humans and dogs, as the concentration of vitamin A is lethally high.

160 An Inuk maneuvers through the pack-ice breaking up off the coast of Grise Fjord, a village on the southern coast of Ellesmere Island in the Canadian archipelago. He is wearing bearskin hunting trousers and impermeable seal-skin boots.

160-161 Two Greenland hunters, keeping their noise to a minimum, crawl up to a group of walruses, who merely watch them. To the delight of bears and foxes, once the animals are killed and deprived of their valuable tusks, their corpses will be abandoned.

case of calamity or for purposes of health care. World War II resulted in an extraordinary upheaval in the Northern territories. Weather stations, airfields, food and munitions deposits and military bases were set up everywhere. Many local inhabitants participated in these operations. They proved to be quite skilled and gave the new arrivals extremely helpful suggestions based on their experience in the region.

At the end of the war, many facilities were abandoned, and the shadow of an economic crisis threatened all those communities that had begun to grow accustomed to another way of life. But a second economic boom again shook the Arctic. When the agreement between the Allies came to an end, the United States and the Soviet Union found themselves in the middle of the Cold War. From Greenland to the Bering Strait, the DEW LINE, or Distant Early Warning Line, was built at a cost of over 600 million dollars, affecting areas that World War II had left untouched. New ports, airports, roads, electric power stations and hospitals were built. About one third of the indigenous population found employment in the colossal operations, and many earned more than $100 a week. When at least some of the reasons for the gigantic build-up ceased to exist as new relationships were built between Russia and the West, almost all local personnel found themselves unemployed. But a return to the primitive lifestyle shaken by these events, which had changed the mentality of an entire generation, proved to be impossible.

The governments on which the Eskimo communities depended increased the benefits of Western progress to the civilian area: schools, health centers and old-age homes were built, and the indigenous populations were offered new job opportunities that encouraged them to build a new artisan culture based on old traditional models. The materials included carved walrus ivory, steatite for large sculptures and tooled skins. The results of these artistic endeavors exceeded all expectations. The works, almost always one of a kind, are prized by tourists, and the finest items are now on display in major museums throughout the world.

162 top After catching a whale using a traditional umiak, which can be seen in the background, the Inuit of northern Alaska try to lift its body onto the pack-ice near Barrow. Today, only the Inuit are allowed to hunt whales, which had been killed in mass numbers up to only a few years ago, bringing them to the brink of extinction.

162 bottom A male narwhal has been caught on the coast of Baffin Island. This cetacean is highly valued for its long, spiral-shaped ivory tooth, which fetches high prices. Its skin is also an excellent source of vitamin C, and the Inuit eat it raw in small quantities as an indispensable dietary supplement.

163 A Chukchi hunter on the Lorinom whaling team in northeastern Siberia throws his heavy harpoon, striking an adult gray whale. Lorinom is on the coast of the Bering Strait, the closest point to Alaska.

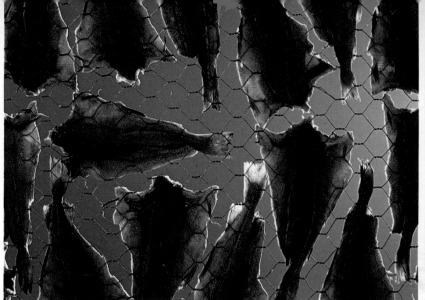

At the same time, the government used every means possible to encourage indigenous groups to concentrate in larger residential clusters so that they could all benefit from hospital and school services. A visitor to Yellowknife, Fairbanks or even Inuvik, the newest of the three towns, will be surprised at the modern variety of merchandise in the supermarkets, the efficiency of the machine shops and the quality of medical care. Schools have one computer for every three students, and in more isolated communities students can take courses by satellite television, sending in questions and answers via radio.

Tourism is also developing beyond all expectations, with new hotels opening every year. Alaska is the preferred destination as it is part of the United States. The majority of visitors come from Seattle via Anchorage or Juneau. In Canada, on the other hand, trips to the Far North are still considered something for the élite. Distances are so great and towns are so scattered that the only way to reach them is by air. At present, there is regular air service to a large network of northern locations, including Resolute on Cornwallis Island at 70° North, which is an important link for small aircraft flying to towns even farther north.

Traveling in one of these planes, almost all of which are single-engine craft, is almost like flying with a bush pilot, one of those fearless aviators who have crossed the bush for half a century, flying by sight across uninhabited, unfamiliar territory without any ground assistance. Like the gold diggers of the Klondike and Nome and the trappers who roamed alone for months in distant, unexplored territories, Alaskan and Canadian bush pilots are part of the epic of the great North.

Travel by dogsled is increasingly rare and has been replaced by fast motorsleds. Wooden or plastic boats have taken the place of kayaks and umjaks, and the traditional igloos and peat structures have been replaced by solid prefabricated wood houses.

With conversion to Christianity, the memory of shamans and ancient animistic beliefs is vanishing. The life that Arctic peoples led for

thousands of years was hard, full of risks and danger, subject to famine caused by unpredictable seasons; the Eskimos' victory over such a hostile environment cost them many human lives. Yet the introduction of fire-arms and mechanical transport alone were not enough to turn the new generation back to their ancient subsistence lifestyle. Moreover, many animals, including the caribou and the whales, have become rare. The fur trade has been stagnant for some time, both because world opinion is against the killing of wild animals and because the Russians have established enormous fur animal breeding centers that now provide these furs.

In the meantime, advances in health care have caused the population to grow everywhere, especially in Alaska. The rejection of the old way of life has been more necessary than voluntary. The Eskimos have great manual skills and have proved to be extremely intelligent, and they can now find employment as specialized workers, tour operators, guides for hunting and fishing parties, skilled artists, and government or community officials.

168 top Pond Inlet is on the northern side of Baffin Island in the Canadian archipelago. It is separated from Bylot Island by Eclipse Sound.

168 center At Igloolik, located on a little island near the coast of Melville Peninsula in the Keewatin district of Canada, an Inuit family has set a bearskin out to dry after having removed the fat. Later, the skin will be stretched on a frame if it is to be sold as it is, or else it will be cut into men's trousers and boot soles. Also note the seal-skin, already stretched out on a frame.

168 bottom Two Inuit women from the Igloolik population walk through the town of the same name.

168-169 Igloolik is a village of about 800 inhabitants located on a little island not far from Melville Peninsula in the Canadian Arctic, in Foxe Basin at the northern tip of Hudson Bay.

Despite the generation shock and the difficulties of such a sudden change, a large, rich country in which new mineral discoveries or energy sources are officially claimed every month cannot help but find a dignified place for a people with such an ancient heritage of patience, tenacity, and honesty, and cannot help but make a positive contribution to the great work of transforming the North. These words may seem bitter to those who have gained a sentimental or romantic view of the old Eskimo world from books or documentaries. Nevertheless, today there are still small enclaves of indigenous peoples, both in northern Greenland and near Point Barrow, Alaska, where cetaceans and pinnipeds are still hunted using traditional methods. In our increasingly technical modern society, there are fortunately still those who have refused to bow to the new collective rites, savoring instead ancient emotions and forgotten flavors.

In Greenland, where a Danish settlement dates back to the time of the missionary Hans Egede, who first began to baptize indigenous peoples in 1721, the transition from the Eskimos' traditional life to the current structure based on the Danish political model was much less traumatic and painful than in North America. Graceful, orderly Scandinavian-style houses have replaced the old, unsanitary dwellings; schools, health centers, hospitals and hospices were built long ago in every town, and those who were still living in small, isolated villages in the 1940's were asked to move to larger communities in order to receive health care and educational benefits.

The most important towns were established and grew up near fish and crustacean processing plants or mining areas, and in the southern part of the country even cattle and sheep breeding was successfully established. There were never any boom and economic recession periods, and small, industrious Denmark with its paternalistic policy based less on technological innovation than on patience and time, has created a present generation of perfectly integrated Danes and native peoples. This is because the integration process was slow and gradual, resulting in far fewer problems than in American and Canadian communities.

169 top Three sealskins have been stretched out on three frames in front of a hunter's house. Also note the snowmobile or skidoo, which has almost completely replaced sled dogs.

170 A member of the Reindeer Chukchi population was photographed after participating in the annual culling of his herd, when old, wounded or sick animals are slaughtered. The absence of snow on the ground and the condition of the reindeer's antlers, which are beginning to shed their velvety covering, are indications that this is the month of August, before the rutting season.

170-171 A herd of reindeer is gathered in a large corral. A Yakut rides a sturdy reindeer as he selects various animals. The migration of reindeer in Eurasia never becomes the massive, long-distance phenomenon of wild caribou in Canada.

171 top left Throughout the Yakut Republic, a pastoral economy linked to reindeer breeding provides the people's basic livelihood. This photo shows a breeder in a corral where animals have been gathered to be marked and branded.

Unlike the wild herds of caribou in Canada, which make two migrations a year, in spring and autumn, in Asia the animals are often limited to a slow wandering of the territory where the owner or herders live.

171 top right A Yakut woman selects several sturdy males to use for riding and as beasts of burden. The animals are castrated and trained for a long period of time before they will obey orders from humans. Sleds are rarely used by Yakuts to transport loads, because in the winter, when their use is feasible, these peoples live sedentary lives.

With respect to Russian Arctic, the great historical changes, the advent of new regimes and their eventual disintegration, all over a relatively brief period of 80 years, have apparently not measurably affected the customs of the peoples of southern Siberia.

The Nentsky, the Samoyed, the Yakuts, the Evenians, the Yukagiri and the Chukchi are still herders and own at least 4 million reindeer. With the advent of communism, steps were quickly taken to Sovietize Siberian activities, but several large herds remained the property of a few communities, and in general during the transition from one regime to another there were no cruel episodes like those that occurred west of the Urals, when the kulaks, or peasant class, were exterminated.

While the communist regime expended every effort to exploit the wealth of Siberia, sending swarms of technicians and workers from the west, the local peoples were left relatively undisturbed to continue their usual lives, with a limited transition from their ancient customs to modern techniques. The only large railway, the Trans-Siberian that connects Moscow to the

Pacific Ocean, runs much farther south, and modern civilization stops a few dozen or at the most a few hundred miles from the various cities it touches along its way. Rivers, on the other hand, have been extremely important for the sale and trade of products, and unlike the Canadian North, which is limited to the Mackenzie River basin, Siberia offers a large number of navigable rivers that run from inland regions to the Arctic Sea. River traffic, which had already reached a million tons by the 1960's, has now doubled.

Of course, Siberian rivers are subject to seasonal limitations that make them navigable only 3-4 months a year, but nevertheless, all the cities which have rapidly developed in the past century are located at or near the mouths of the largest rivers. Salekhard is at the mouth of the Ob, Dundinka, Norilsk and Dikson are at the mouth of the Ienissei, Nordvik is at the mouth of the Khatanga and Tiksi is at the mouth of the Lena. Anadyr is on the Pacific coast, at the mouth of the Anadyr River. In all these cities, the population is 50% Russian and 50% indigenous. While the bigger cities show the marks of Soviet centralized urbanization, with large 2-3-story elongated buildings that look like barracks, in the smaller towns the yaranda and yurt are still in use.

These are traditional circular structures built with an elaborate framework of flexible, interwoven branches covered with reindeer hide stitched together and placed on top.

These dwellings were used by nomadic herders, who built one permanent wooden house in the forest and another portable house they could travel with. The large numbers of animals are of great material and strategic value and provide many people with everything they need.

The movements of the great herds are now controlled by helicopters and small airplanes, and a good veterinary service has been introduced. In addition to reindeer, many Arctic foxes and minks are raised in the Chukchi Peninsula, where food for them comes almost entirely from the sea. In recent years Chukchi crafts have conquered the Alaska side of the Bering Strait, and due to profitable exchanges with Americans this community is

172 top left The Khants and Mansi live just east of the Ural Mountains. The semi-nomadic Khants are more numerous, while there are only a little over a thousand Mansi, with an accurate census made extremely difficult by the fact that they are totally nomadic. The two populations live in close contact within the same territory and have almost exactly the same lifestyle, making it very difficult to distinguish them. The economy of both peoples is closely bound to reindeer herding. This child in the photo is sitting on a sled waiting for the tent to be built.

172 bottom left The wide tent has been completed. Note that smoke does not issue from the hole in the center, but from a special tube.

172 right Katya, a young twenty-year old woman wearing a bright red outfit, is busy unloading baggage from the sled.

173 This is the interior of a permanent structure. Note the clearly Mongoloid features of the woman, as well as her clothing, similar to that worn by the Tungus, a people who live thousands of miles away.

174 top This is a young Chukchi from Uelen, a village on the north coast of the Chukchi Peninsula, not far from the Bering Strait. The village is now quite popular with American tourists, often accompanied by dogs and sleds. Dogsled racing, which is quite popular in Alaska, the home of the most famous world competitions, is now also practiced in the nearby Chukchi Peninsula.

175 top left Chukchi women from Lorinom chop a gray whale (Eschrichtus robustus). This species is one of the few left in the Arctic after the heedless slaughter of larger species.

175 top right Whalers from Lorinom who have caught a narwhal quickly swallow raw pieces of skin after sectioning the tail. This animal's skin is a source of vitamin C, and young people in particular are urged to eat it.

174 bottom An old Chukchi smokes a cigarette in a handmade cigarette holder. The Chukchi skilled craftsmen use walrus teeth as a raw material, decorated whole or carved to make small objects. While these handicrafts once went to markets in Moscow, now most of them go to Alaska.

174-175 A Lorinom hunter carries two walruses on his motor boat; he will use the precious tusks, the skin and the fat. Walruses are particularly numerous throughout the Chukchi Peninsula.

becoming different from other Arctic regions. We should finally note that, despite the heavy criticism that can be leveled against the Soviet system, the USSR was the only country to give the various local ethnic groups their own independent republics, with Parliamentary representatives in Moscow and equal voting rights. Indeed, the Eskimo and Indian ethnic groups in Alaska and Canada have never received any recognition in government.

Only in recent years, in addition to the appointment of a Parliamentary representative for their territories, have the Canadian communities been granted any share in the economic benefits gained through the exploitation of mineral and energy resources.

Greenland recently gained formal independence with self-governance. Here, however, the Eskimos, or more accurately the Greenlanders, have interbred with the Danes for many years and have even lost many of their original Mongol characteristics. In any event, the island was a Danish colony for so long that extensive cultural and commercial ties with the mother country still exist, and Danish is even the official language in relations with other countries. While independence has created no problem in Greenland's relationships with the United States, which maintains a big military base at Thule, independence created a serious problem in relations with the European Community because the fishing waters of the big island are no more freely accessible to all of them.

The situation is now even worse because the progressive increase in water temperatures in the North Atlantic has resulted in increasingly numerous schools of fish along Greenland's shores. The European Community has made efforts to resolve this pressing question, with Denmark acting as mediator: individual concessions which are quite lucrative for Greenland have already been made.

176 top and 176-177 A group of Yakuts with Mongolian features and brightly-colored costumes on their way to a local festival. The photos were taken in sub-arctic Siberia. In the winter this region is the coldest place in Asia. The photo also shows many Russians, lured here, over 3,000 miles from Russian Europe, in search of new mining and industrial opportunities by the expansion eastward.

177 top left A pair of reindeer are prepared for sacrifice in a propitiatory ceremony known as the Turum festival, practiced by the Yakuts.

177 top right The faces and garments of these Yakut women reveal their Mongolian origins.

178 top Unexpectedly emerging from the water, a humpback whale (Megaptera novaslingliae) frightens seagulls intent on catching surface krill.

178 bottom This photo shows a parade of humpback whales as they emerge from the water together. These whales, one of the few species that can still be seen in the Arctic, are social and playful, and they indulge in jumps and displays that seem to have no other purpose than their pleasure.

LIFE ABOVE AND BELOW THE ICE

178-179 The humpback whale has enormous ventral fins and numerous warts around its mouth, which are often attacked by parasitic invertebrates. These whales are often hunted by orcas, who attack them in groups and bite at their large fins, which make an easy target.

179 top left The sperm whale (Phisiter macrocephalus), whose tail is visible here, is a toothed whale. It only has teeth on the lower jaw, which is long and narrow, while the upper jaw is toothless. It is nevertheless very efficient in catching the cuttlefish and giant squid on which it feeds, swimming at great depths.

179 top right Humpback whales can leap acrobatically out of the water; this skill is clearly seen in the picture. This is one of the slowest-swimming whales, which makes it easier to hunt.

Arctic plants and animals can be broken down into a number of communities which are related in various ways. The most important relationship involves the formation of plankton, the one-celled plants (phytoplankton) or minuscule crustaceans (zooplankton) on which Arctic creatures feed. In the summer, the plankton moves to the surface areas of the sea, and all other marine creatures depend on it for life, as it serves as nourishment for gigantic whalebone whales, which ingest it directly.

The phytoplankton floats, carried by the marine currents, and utilizes sunlight to grow and multiply, producing nutritious material by means of chlorophyll photosynthesis. The long days of May and June stimulate the phytoplankton to grow rapidly, and the zooplankton takes advantage of this abundance by growing and increasing in turn, forming large banks that extend for many miles in the Arctic, and even farther in the Antarctic.

Fish, mollusks, cephalopods, pinnipeds and cetaceans, known as nekton, live in both surface and deep waters, depending on the season and the availability of nourishment.

Polar waters are not particularly rich in nutritive salts but do contain oxygen. When the waters of the Atlantic and the Pacific meet Arctic waters, they create excellent conditions for the development of plankton, resulting in a true explosion of life at all levels. Various surface crustaceans and many fish, the most common of which are herring and *Mallotus villosus*, form large schools that follow the swarms of plankton. These schools attract other fish like mackerel and cod, as well as flocks of birds, pinnipeds and toothed whales. In their turn, humans catch great quantities of fish, mammals and birds; recently even zooplankton has been canned for human consumption in Japan, Korea and Russia, where it is an ingredient in feed for many animals.

Because it has direct repercussions on many marine species and birds, the significant increase in temperature in the North Atlantic over the past 50 years is an important phenomenon. Temperatures have risen about 2° C, with immediate effects on the exchange with polar waters. Greenland and Iceland in particular have benefited, and their catch of cod, halibut and whiting has continued to increase.

The same holds for the basking shark *(Ceterhinus maximus)*, up to 17 feet long, which has now become common prey in the waters between Greenland and the Svalbards. With their gigantic size and legendary fame, cetaceans are the animals which most capture human fantasy. Cetaceans were once land animals which transformed into sea creatures over the course of millions of years, becoming perfectly streamlined and developing a heavy layer of subcutaneous fat.

They include some of the largest mammals on the Earth, and despite merciless, indiscriminate slaughter by man over the past three centuries (it is estimated that almost 2 million cetaceans have been killed), several cetaceans have survived. With luck, they can still be seen swimming in the sea or in the areas where they gather to give birth or mate.

This class of mammals is divided into two families, both of which are well-represented in the Arctic: the *Mysticeti*, or true whales, which have no teeth, and the *Odontoceti*, which have teeth. The first are large animals up to 100 feet in length which use whalebone to filter the plankton-rich waters. The whalebone imbedded on the palate works like large, extremely fine combs which can hold in even tiny solid particles.

Toothed cetaceans, including the popular dolphins and porpoises, are generally smaller. The only exception is the sperm whale *(Phisiter catodon)*, which may reach 70 feet in length. The orcas too *(Orcinus orca)* are also large and can reach up to 35 feet in length. Orcas, which are members of the dolphin family, have a milky-colored body dappled with black, and powerful teeth. These gregarious creatures are the most ferocious of cetaceans, and will gather in groups of 10-20 individuals to attack any sort of prey, including rorquals, humpback whales, seals, or sea lions, and will even invade and decimate schools of dolphins.

In captivity, they are always quite friendly to humans and behave like the bottle-nosed dolphin *(Tursiops truncatus)* and the porpoise *(Phocaena phocaena)*, which are well-known in dolphin aquariums throughout the world. Other important cetaceans that live in the Arctic include the beluga or white whale *(Delphinapterus leucas)*, which reaches over 16 feet in length, and the narwhal *(Monodon monoceros)*, which is just as large, with males of the species sporting a long spiral-shaped beak-like rostrum, the result of the abnormal growth of the upper left incisor.

This species is particularly interesting for a number of reasons: a) it is the only cetacean that lives in Arctic waters all year round; as it must live in the dark for months, its vision is weak, but it has a strong eco-sensory organ that guides it perfectly; b) its skin is rich in vitamin C, and the coastal Eskimos have always taken advantage of this unique vitamin source; c) it has two permanent gathering areas in the late spring: a fjord not far from Thule in Greenland, and Lancaster Sound, thus making it easy for local hunters to make their (limited) catch.

The sperm whale is the deepest-swimming cetacean, diving down to over 1200 feet and beyond. Its narrow lower jaw armed with formidable teeth (the upper jaw has no teeth) allows it to catch slippery cuttlefish and giant squid. There is a large reserve of white, odorless oil in the enormous head of this cetacean and a round, waxy, grayish substance called

182 top This photo shows an exceptional concentration of belugas or white whales (Delphinapterus leucae) at the mouth of the Cunningham River on Baffin Island. This toothed whale is similar in form to the pilot whale.

182 center Three male narwhals (Monodon monoceros) swim in a channel which has opened in the pack-ice near Baffin Island in the Canadian archipelago.

182 bottom A beluga whale maneuvering near the coast of Somerset Island in the Canadian archipelago. This cetacean is the same size as the narwhal, 16 feet from the tip of the snout to the end of the tail, and often accompanies it.

182-183 The Arctic coastal populations value the beluga and hunt it for its fat, which until recently was used to produce light and heat. It is now one of the most numerous cetaceans, as its relatively modest size saved it from the destructive fury of ocean-going whalers.

ambragrigia; both materials were once valuable for industrial use.

Members of the Mysticeti family include the sei whale *(Balaenoptera borealis)*, which reaches a length of almost 70 feet, the minke whale *(Balaenoptera acutostrata)*, about half the size of the sei whale with characteristic white fins, the gray whale *(Eschrichtius robustus)*, which is rather stocky and 40-45 feet long, the humpback whale *(Megaptera novaeangliae)*, 60 feet long, distinguished by the extremely long fins and the noticeably white belly, and the bowhead whale *(Balaena mysticetus)*, also known as the true whale (60-70 feet long), with an overly large head that occupies one third of the length of its body.

All these cetaceans winter in open waters away from the pack-ice and appear in the late spring in more northerly waters, where they find abundant food. Although the sounds they emit are not as numerous and varied as those in the Odontoceti family, these whales, especially the humpback whale, have a rich repertory of sounds that can be detected by hydrophone. The "songs" of the whales include sounds that distinguish animals of the same group and hunting signals, made when various cetaceans gather to emit sounds and produce air bubbles that carry plankton or small fish to where they can most easily be caught.

All cetaceans reproduce and give birth in the sea. In addition to the above-described class of mammals, which is the most specialized in pelagic life, there is another class of marine mammals with many members in the Arctic: the pinnipeds. Like cetaceans, pinnipeds are carnivorous animals which have adapted to aquatic life.

Unlike cetaceans, however, they reproduce on the ice and the coast, and may spend long periods of time out of the water during the mating and reproduction seasons.

The pinnipeds can be divided into three groups:
1) Odobenidae or walruses
2) Otariidae or sea lions and fur seals
3) Phocidae or seals

The Odobenidae order includes a single species, the walrus *(Odobenus rosmarus)*, a massive, awkward animal (a male may weigh more than 1.5 tons) with a thick, wrinkled skin like the trunk of an old oak, two tusks that look like those of a young elephant, toothbrush whiskers, small eyes and flippers with sharp claws.

*183 top Some beluga
whales are diving in
Lancaster Sound in the
Canadian archipelago,
one of the seasonal
gathering places for
belugas and narwhals*

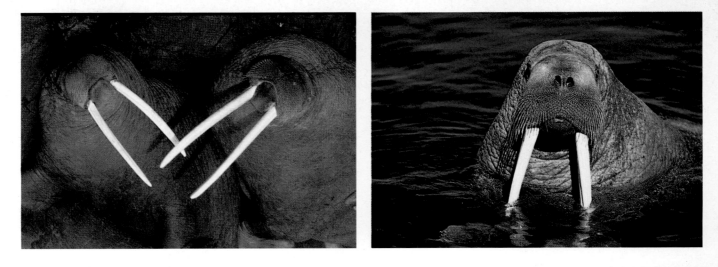

While it is slow and clumsy on land, in the sea it is majestic and elegant and can swim for extraordinarily long periods of time. The function of walrus tusks is still not clearly understood. Some researchers believe that the long teeth are used to remove bivalve mollusks from the sea beds, while others feel that the tusks could be used to make breathing holes in the pack ice.

Walruses often gather in the hundreds to rest in the sun on the beach, becoming a reddish color with the warmth. They are very social creatures and will even risk their own lives to help a wounded companion. Walruses are subject to controlled hunting by Eskimos, in particular for their ivory tusks. Sea lions are members of the Otariidae order, which means "seals with ears." The distinctive characteristics of this order are the small external ears and the testicles enclosed within a scrotal sac, unlike walruses and seals, who have no ears and have testicles in the abdomen. There are two families in the order. The sea lions *(Eumetopias jubatas)* have a rounder head, snub nose and a thick pelt without an undercoat. Males reach about 9 feet in length and may weigh as much as a ton, while females are only one quarter as heavy.

The fur seals *(Callorhinus ursinus)* have a more elegant head, more pointed nose and fur that includes a thick, soft undercoat. Males in this family reach 7 feet in length and weigh from 450 to 650 pounds, while females weigh reach 100-140 pounds.

The great sexual differences in pinnipeds is a constant characteristic in all animals which live in harems, where males try to keep numerous females and their pups under control. As sea lions and fur seals have no layer of fat to protect them from the cold, unlike walruses and seals they avoid swimming in waters which could be covered with drift ice, and only males who have finished mating travel as far north as the Bering Strait. Fur seals were hunted indiscriminately until early in the 20th century, almost to the verge of extinction. Now the species is protected and is beginning to recover.

The nine genera of seals which live in the Arctic live in different areas. Of these, three genera are truly Arctic, as they live in waters which are covered with ice all year round. They are the first three mentioned on our list.

186 top The photo shows the head of a bearded seal (Erignatus barbatus). This is one of the largest species of seal and may reach a length of 6 to 10 feet and a weight of 600 pounds. Its fur looks silky, with reddish-brown highlights. Its thick whiskers act as vibrissae and are used to find food on the sea floor.

186-187 Two walruses swim in the frigid waters of Southhampton Island at the northern tip of Hudson Bay in eastern Canada. These pinnipeds become gray when it is cold and turn bright pink when they warm up on the rocks in the sun.

1) The spotted seal (Phoca largha) lives in the Chukchi Sea and never descends below the Bering Strait.

2) The ringed seal (Phoca hispida) lives near Greenland down to the Svalbard Islands. It is very common and is not only hunted by the Eskimos, but is also the polar bear's favorite prey.

3) The bearded seal (Ergnatus barbatus) is quite large and has thick whiskers. It lives in Greenland and the Canadian archipelago.

4) The harbor seal (Phoca vitulina) is quite common from the waters of Norway to those of America.

5) The harp seal (Phoca groenlandica) is common from Hudson Bay to Novaya Zemlya. Its name comes from the strange design on its back, which looks like a Celtic harp. Because it is pure white at birth, this seal was ruthlessly hunted for its fur, and only in recent years has it been placed under protection.

6) The ribbon seal (Phoca fasciata) has white and dark brown rings on its fur and lives exclusively in the northern Pacific, down to the Bering Strait.

7) The gray seal (Halichoemus gripsus) lives between Iceland and Newfoundland.

8) The bladdernose seal (Cystophora crestata) is larger than other seals and is distinguished by a noticeable protuberance on the nose of males, which they can swell by making a loud noise, apparently as a mating call or territorial signal.

9) The elephant seal (Mironga angustirostris) is a true giant which is fairly common in the northern Pacific, where it lives as far down as the Bering Strait. Its name comes from the long protuberance on the nose that can be filled with air and used as a resounding chamber for issuing mighty roars. Only a few animals live in the Arctic year-round. They belong to families which originated farther south and developed special defenses against the cold, enabling them to survive in the harshest climate on Earth. Apart from 13 land mammals, 3 pinnipeds, 1 cetacean and 4 birds, all animals are migratory.

The polar bear (Thalarctos maritimus) is the largest of the great land carnivores, although it lives most of its life on floating ice and in the sea. To protect it against the cold, it has a thick oily fur which is pure white at birth but tends to become light yellow as it ages, and a thick layer of subcutaneous fat. This reserve of fat allows it to live for up to 3-4 months with little food. Even the pads on its paws have fur, which not only protects it from the cold but effectively grips even slick ice. The polar bear does not go into hibernation like its southern relatives, but roams and swims tirelessly all year round. One bear was found in the open sea more than 30 miles from the nearest land or pack ice, another was sighted by the crew of the nuclear submarine Skate as it emerged at the North Pole, and a bear tagged by a group of researchers was found the next year almost 2,000 miles away.

The bear is a solitary animal: the female (but not the male) lives with her newborn cubs for about two years, teaching them how to hunt and defending them from male bears. This animal is extraordinarily strong and can kill an adult seal with a single swipe of its paw. On land, it is faster than man and can run 25 miles an hour. Today limited numbers of polar bears can be hunted exclusively by Arctic coastal populations such as Eskimos and the Chukchi. It is estimated that there are 20,000-25,000 polar bears in existence. Many can be seen each year near the city of Churchill, Canada, on the Hudson Bay.

The Arctic wolf (Canis lupus arctos) lives in the northern part of the Canadian archipelago, especially on Ellesmere Island, where packs of wolves hunt musk oxen and Peary caribou. As protection against the cold, the wolf has a double layer of fur consisting of longer outer hairs and a dense, woolly undercoat.

Like the polar bear, the Arctic wolf has insulating fur on the pads of its paws. If the animal is caught in a storm away from its den, it curls up and covers its nose and ears with its thick tail, allowing itself to be completely buried in the snow. Its ears are smaller and more rounded than those of its more southern cousins. The Arctic wolf keeps its white coat all year round. The male is an affectionate father and cooperates generously with his lifetime female companion in hunting food for their pups. Pups are born in litters of 4-7 and begin to grow independent at around 6 months old. Arctic wolves also hunt Arctic hares and lemmings.

Zoologists have long been uncertain how to classify the musk ox (Ovibos muschatus), and this is evident in its scientific name (Ovibos literally means "sheep-ox"). Its strong musk odor is due

188 top left The female bladdernose seal (Cystophora crystata) is an extremely protective and aggressive mother and allows no one to approach her young. This is a large species; males reach a length of 7 feet and a weight of over 800 pounds. Males have a fleshy appendage on the

nose which can be expanded to emit a sort of roar, used both as a mating call and a territorial signal. This seal lives off Labrador, in Greenland and on Jan Mayen Island.

188 top right The gray seal (Halichoerus grypsus) is over 8 feet

long and is common on the Atlantic coasts between Newfoundland and Iceland. A large colony is also present on the Baltic Sea. This species feeds on fish, crustaceans and cuttlefish and hunts both by day and at night. Its calls are much louder than those of other seals and can be heard for many miles.

188-189 and 189 The harbor seal (Phoca vitulina) is one of the smallest species, reaching a length of 4-7 feet and a weight of 200-400 pounds. This species is common in Hudson Bay, Labrador, Greenland, Iceland, the British Isles and the Baltic Sea. Its mantle is blue-gray with dark and black spots. It feeds on seabed fish and mollusks.

to special scent glands near its eyes. It has a stubby body which is protected by a thick coat of fur consisting of longer hairs and an undercoat of very fine wool (finer and more valuable than the finest cashmere). It has a long beard that connects to the fur that hangs from its neck and flanks. Its tail is short. Its legs are typically sheep-like and end in a very large, robust hoof which allows the animal to walk easily on the snow and is an effective tool for digging into the frozen ground in search of food, primarily dwarf shrubs. The musk ox usually lives in groups which gather together in case of danger, forming a protective shield, with the strongest males on the outside and the smaller or weaker animals within. This has facilitated their decimation by humans, who can easily shoot an entire group gathered this way. The wolf, its other implacable predator, uses various diversionary tactics to make the herd lose patience and abandon its defensive position, thus leaving isolated animals at the mercy of the predator.

The Peary caribou *(Rangifer arcticus pearyi)* is the smallest of the caribou in the Canadian Arctic. Unlike more southern species, it does not migrate south to the taiga in the autumn, nor does it move north in the spring. Its habitat is the most northerly islands in the Canadian archipelago, where the vegetation is sparse and its nourishment is reduced to mosses and lichens. Unlike continental caribou, which are brownish-gray, Peary caribou, which live in Greenland as well, are white or very light gray. Its fur is even thicker than that of its southern cousins and does not thin out much in the summer. Its shorter legs and wider hooves make it less elegant than other caribou, but its body is well-adapted to living in high latitudes. Finally, it is not as disturbed by summer insects as southern caribou are, as the ponds and little lakes where it lives are frozen for most of the year and offer no place for insect larvae.

The Arctic fox *(Alopex lagopus)* has a shorter body, less pointed snout, and much smaller ears than the red fox, and has a white coat all year round. Its range is extremely wide, at the edge of the taiga up to a latitude of 83° North, where it follows polar bears in order to feed on their leftovers. It also hunts Arctic hares, various other hares, lemmings, voles and Arctic ground

squirrels. In the summer it adds eggs and nestlings to its diet. Its fur is quite valuable, and like that of the Arctic wolf consists of longer fur and an undercoat. These foxes are not afraid of humans, and they have raided many an explorer's tents and provisions. A blue-gray variety of the Arctic fox is rather common. Its morphology and habits are identical to the pure-white variety.

The Arctic hare *(Lepus arcticus)* has specifically northern features that distinguish it from its more southern cousins and enable it to survive in the north. Its ears are shorter, its snout rounder, its legs have wider paws that allow it to walk in deep snow, and its coat is completely white except for the tips of its ears. It eats small shrubs, which it chews for some time to make them tender. Its young have brown fur which blends perfectly with the color of the tundra. Its enemies include the wolf, the fox, the ermine, the weasel and the snow owl.

The ermine *(Mustela erminea)* is a small but formidable hunter which is active both summer and winter. During the summer it enters the dens of lemmings and voles, creating havoc. In the winter, when small mammals dig tunnels under

the snow, its excellent hearing helps it to locate them easily. In the summer it feeds on eggs, nestlings, ground squirrels and even hares, which are much larger than it is. At high latitudes, the ermine has a white coat all year round, except for the black tip of its tail. Quite sought-after for its fur and hunted for many years, it has nevertheless not suffered irreparable losses and is still quite common. In lower latitudes to the edge of the taiga, the ermine is brown, with a lighter colored lower part of the body.

The least weasel *(Mustela nivalis)* is a little smaller than the ermine and has similar habits. It has shorter fur but is just as active and agile as the ermine. In general it lives farther south than the ermine, reaching the edge of the taiga in winter. The weasel also has a pure-white coat, but only during the winter. Its tail is also completely white. In addition to lemmings and voles, weasels eat eggs and nestlings and will sometimes attack young hares.

There are two types of lemmings: the Arctic or collared lemming *(Dicrostonyx groenlandicus)* and the brown lemming *(Lemmus trimucronatus)*. The former is the Eurasian variety, while the latter is North American. In a certain sense, lemmings are the first link in the Western food chain, as they are preyed upon by all carnivorous mammals and raptors. In the winter this small herbivore is hunted only by the ermine and the weasel, who slip into the tunnels they dig under the snow. To combat this massive, ceaseless slaughter, lemmings are amazingly prolific; the first matings occur in March and may be repeated 4-5 times a year. As the newborn lemmings are sexually mature at 3 months, 500 lemmings can be produced by the first pair and its progeny in just one year. A similar proliferation may take place when weather conditions are favorable. If the winter is long, with no abundant plants and leaves, lemming births decrease, and thus food becomes scarce for predators as well, who will also produce fewer young.

Recent observations have revealed that this lemming birth cycle is not totally dependent on environmental conditions, but rather follows a four-year pattern which in its turn influences the number of predators. The legend that lemmings will intentionally drown themselves when the

population grows too large is untrue. What actually happens is that when the territory is saturated with a certain population, the lemmings move in dense groups in search of less crowded areas. As they move in compact formation in a predetermined, fixed direction, the horde of lemmings may encounter rivers or lakes which they are unable to cross, and thus tens of thousands of them may drown. Lemmings are small animals, and only the Groenlandian variety becomes white in the winter. During other seasons these small mammals with their rounded bodies and barely visible tails have colors which mimic the tundra where they live.

The ground squirrel *(Citellus undulatus)* is not as common on the tundra as the lemming. In general, it prefers drier areas which are not too far from water. Ground squirrels are light brown all year long, and unlike lemmings they go into hibernation in a communal den which houses many members of the group. In the spring, when the den no longer offers protection, ground squirrels are hunted by all Arctic carnivores, especially the fox.

The red-backed vole *(Clethrionomys gapperi)* is another very small animal. It has colors that mimic its surroundings like the lemmings. Its tail is much shorter than in southern species of voles. This small mammal also lives in long, complex burrows during the summer and in tunnels under the snow in the winter. Its habits are quite similar to the lemming, and like it, it is extremely prolific, although this can fluctuate over time.

The masked shrew *(Sorex cinereus)* is the smallest mammal that winters in the Arctic. It is always searching for insects, larvae and worms and lives in burrows which are as small as its tiny body. This makes it impossible for the usual predators to enter. When the shrew leaves its burrow, however, it is easy prey for all carnivores.

Birds which winter in the Arctic are just as few as the mammals, if not fewer, and belong to quite different orders.

The snow owl *(Nyctea scandiaca)* is large (2 feet tall) and has completely white plumage, except for a few small brown spots on the wings. Even its legs are covered with thick plumage, leaving only its claws visible. Its eyes, which are round as in other owls, are covered by a white lid

194 top left The polar bear (Thalartos maritimus) *moves tirelessly throughout the Arctic, at ease both on the ice and in the water. Its thick layer of subcutaneous fat and its oily fur protect it from cold and humidity.*

194 top right A female with her young does not hesitate to cross a wide arm of the sea here at Wager Bay, in the Keewatin district not far from the northwest tip of Hudson Bay.

that makes the Arctic variety unmistakable. It also has no auricular tuft. During the summer the snow owl nests on the ground. Its preferred prey are lemmings and voles, as well as young Arctic hares. It usually hunts by day.

The gyrfalcon *(Falcus rusticulus)* is the largest member of the Falconidae family. At high latitudes its plumage is completely white, while those who winter farther south have a speckled brown plumage that makes them look like the peregrine falcon. It flies low, moving to higher elevations when it leaves a familiar area to explore a new territory. It preys on small mammals.

The willow ptarmigan *(Lagopus lagopus)* has a white plumage in winter that makes it completely invisible, while its brownish-red summer plumage also mimics the colors of the tundra quite well. It is the largest of the ptarmigans (about 16 inches tall) and is larger than the ptarmigan found at lower latitudes, for example in the Alps (14 inches tall). The willow ptarmigan feeds on the ground, scratching with its feathered legs in search of seeds, berries, seedlings and insects.

The common raven *(Corvus corax)* has an extraordinary ability to adapt to any latitude. With no apparent morphological differences from those who live in more southern regions, the raven is omnipresent in the Arctic, where it feeds on the remains of any carrion, fish and refuse from human settlements. Arctic peoples consider it intelligent and versatile, and there is no legend or popular belief in any of the Arctic regions which does not consider the raven to be a sacred, magical creature.

The snow bunting *(Plectrophenax nivalis)* is a small bird (5 inches tall) which has no special defenses yet survives all year round in the most northern territories. A member of the chaffinch family, it searches incessantly for food (seeds and berries, even if frozen or dried out) to obtain the necessary calories for survival. The snow bunting has two stomachs (one serves as a food reservoir), but it is still a mystery how such a fragile creature can survive the long winter months. How do sedentary animals in the Arctic survive during the long polar night? Surrounded by ice and darkness, how do they find the resources to overcome the harshest season of the year?

Most of the Arctic regions have no sun for many weeks during the winter. Less snow falls in

194-195 Despite its size and weight, up to a half a ton for males, the polar bear is quite agile and sure-footed on thin or unstable sheets of ice.

195 The polar bear is always at ease both on a fragment of pack-ice or swimming in the open sea. Bears have been sighted 25-30 miles from the nearest land or ice floe. This photo, taken in Franz Joseph Land, in the Russian Arctic, also shows a rare ivory gull (Pagophila ebornea).

these areas than in other more southerly regions, but because the snow cover never melts, almost all of the earth remains permanently covered with snow. A few Arctic willows poke out of the snow, providing food for the willow ptarmigan and hares. The musk oxen and Peary caribou, comfortably warm in their thick winter coats, search for food on higher ground, where the Arctic winds blow stronger and sweep the snow away. The former are content with dry herbs and little shrubs, while the latter prefer mosses and lichens.

Arctic foxes whose acute sense of hearing and smell allow them to identify the movements of small mammals under the snow manage to find fresh prey even in the scarce season. They also find plenty of food when a polar bear abandons the carcass of a seal after eating its fill, or when wolves kill some large mammal. Arctic hares travel in large groups of as many as 100 individuals, in search of frozen shrubs which become tender when chewed for some time.

The polar bear is far away on the vast winter ice-pack, and taking advantage of any small crack the seals open in order to breathe, it finds enough prey to last till the end of winter, when there will be migrating seals in addition to wintering seals to eat. Pregnant females build dens in the snow, but never go into true hibernation. They give birth in January-February, and the seal pups leave the den in March-April, living with their mothers for at least two years. There is greater activity under the snow. The layer of snow acts as insulation, and the temperature at ground level is always 7°-8° warmer than on the outside.

Small mammals, lemmings, voles and shrews winter here, where they survive on the tundra all year round. With the exception of the dark, their lives vary little from summer to winter. Herbivores have easy access to vegetation, while shrews, which are insectivores, find a wide selection of worms, larvae and insects in hibernation. Even the dangers which threaten them are no different from those in the summer: ermines and weasels are quite agile and slender and can slip in under the snow, where they spend most of the winter hunting their usual prey.

Of course, the winter season always claims its victims. Sudden snowstorms followed by intense

196-197 The town of Churchill, in the far north of the province of Manitoba in Canada, lies on the wide Hudson Bay. Each autumn a large number of polar bears gather in this relatively southern area: indeed, Churchill is below the 60° parallel north. For a certain period during the year the animals abandon their customary solitary lives and become more social. Encounters between bears of the same sex always result in a long series of games, feigned combats and ritual gestures, like those shown in these two pages.

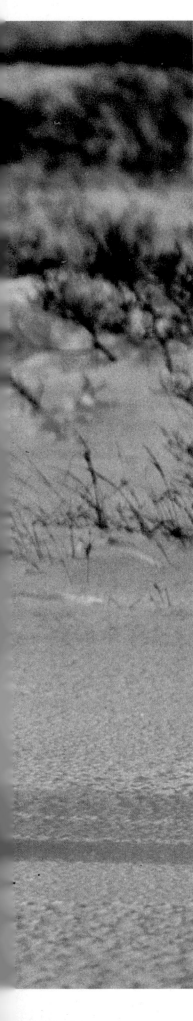

cold prevent small herbivores from reaching their forage, and even carnivores, especially larger ones like bears and wolves, must endure long periods without food, sometimes unbearably long. The return of sunlight means survival for many threatened creatures.

In April the deep winter silence is suddenly broken by the cheerful call of the snow bunting. This little bird is the true harbinger of a spectacular invasion that in only a few weeks' time brings tens of millions of birds to the Arctic, coming from the whole northern hemisphere and beyond.

Of the over 100 varieties of birds that spend the summer in the Arctic, only about a half a dozen are songbirds. In addition to the snow bunting, there is the northern wheatear (*Oenanthe oenanthe*), the meadow pipet (*Anthus pratensis*), the Siberian pipet (*Anthus gustavi*), the water pipet (*Anthus spinoletta*), the horned lark (*Eremophila alpestris*) and the bluethroat (*Luscinia svecica*). As there are no trees to perch on, all these birds sing in flight to defend their territories and search for mates.

But most migratory birds are aquatic and begin to arrive in May. During this month the snow still lies thick on the ground and the ponds are frozen, making their arrival seem premature. But the reproductive season in the far North is brief, and the birds must be ready to mate as soon as they have enough food available. This way they will be able to raise their young before the return migration. A few days later, the whistling swans (*Cygnus cygnus*) arrive in their white plumage and add new grass to last year's nest; these birds always return to the same place. As soon as the ice begins to crack on the lakes and marshes, ducks and loons arrive. Around the first of June the waders make their appearance, quickly followed by the phalaropes. During the same period the Arctic tern (*Sterna paradisaea*), the champion of long distance migrating birds, arrives after a 5,000-5,500 mile flight from the eastern hemisphere. The length of these days makes up for the shortness of the Arctic summer. Working tirelessly, the birds manage to gather enough food to feed larger broods of fledglings than other similar species which live where the days are shorter.

198 top and 199 bottom Two young bears make friends and play in the autumn near Churchill. The pack-ice, still too fragile in autumn, keeps them on land. Within a few weeks the young bears will make their first attempt at hunting equally young seals.

198-199 A female plays with her cubs while keeping a close eye to be sure no males are nearby. When they are hungry, males do not hesitate to attack cubs, and the mother, who will sacrifice her own life for the cubs, does not always succeed in saving them.

199 top A tender family portrait in the Churchill interior: a female uses her own body heat to warm her cubs, born in the previous winter, who will be inseparable from her for another year. In addition to feeding them, the mother gives them their first lessons in hunting.

200-201 The musk ox (Ovibos moschatus) is the ruminant that lives in the farthest North in the Arctic. Musk oxen can be seen on Ellesmere Island in the far north of the Canadian archipelago and in northern Greenland, where the land is free of snow only three months a year. Using its heavy hooves, musk oxen can dig out food from under the snow, consisting of moss, grasses and leaves of dwarf shrubs. Unlike caribou, it will only rarely eat lichens. Its fur consists of long, coarse hair and an undercoat of fine wool that insulates against the cold Arctic temperatures. In the summer it molts quite visibly. Musk oxen always live in herds of 10-15 individuals. When attacked, they defend themselves by making a compact formation, with the strongest males on the outside protecting the younger and weaker animals within. Unfortunately, musk oxen gathered together like this make it easy for humans to kill in the group. Timber wolves (Canis Lupus Arctos), which are also implacable enemies of musk oxen, use a different technique, tiring the herd with repeated attacks from every direction, finally driving the compact group apart and attacking the weakest, isolated individuals. The musk oxen here were photographed on Univak Island in the Bering Sea off the west coast of Alaska.

While these great migrations are taking place, another massive land migration is under way, calling hundreds of thousands of caribou *(Rangifer tarandus)* from the forests at the edge of the tundra, where they have sought refuge during the winter, to the shores of the Arctic sea. At one time, before indiscriminate slaughter decimated the herds of these deer, it is estimated that there were 20 to 25 million of them in Canadian territory. They now seem to have stabilized at 500,000-600,000. The caribou is an animal that reaches 5 feet at the withers and may weigh from 500-700 pounds. Its wide hooves support it well both on the sodden, spongy ground in spring and on the winter snow. It is quite robust and can even dig for food under the snow. Caribou feed exclusively on lichens and certain mosses, present everywhere along their migration route north. In the winter while they are in the forests, caribou will even pull moss and lichens from tree trunks. Caribou can gallop at a speed of almost 40 miles an hour, especially when pursued by wolves, and can swim quite well when water invades their path.

Males and females have magnificent branched antlers covered with a velvety brown skin, irrigated with dense blood vessels that keep the animal cool during the summer. Later, this covering falls off, and the antlers become a weapon for males contending for females. Males lose their antlers in December-January, and the females about a month later. In April the antlers of both males and females grow back, and the females give birth between April and May. Their young are immediately capable of following the adults in their wanderings. Once they have completed their long migratory route, the caribou break up into groups of 100-150 individuals. In the summer they prefer high areas well-exposed to the wind which provide maximum protection against insects. As autumn arrives, the herds gather into large groups, and the caribou head for another long voyage south to the forests of the taiga, where they are less exposed to the winter winds.

The reindeer is the Eurasian equivalent of the caribou. It is smaller, with a height of 3 feet at the withers and a weight of 200-300 pounds. Although wild reindeer no longer exist, their wanderings are almost as free as those of their

202-203 An Arctic fox
(Alopex lagopus) *moves*
warily across the
disintegrating pack-ice.
The Arctic fox has a
shorter muzzle than the
red fox (Vulpes fulva),
with a more compact
body, smaller ears and
bushier tail. It is also
smaller in size, reaching
a maximum of 14-18
pounds.

American cousins: each year they cross the tundra from south to north and back again, following the rhythm of the seasons under the supervision of guardians who often own the herds. The species is common from Norway to the Chukchi Peninsula, and the economy of many peoples is still based on reindeer breeding.

The rough fur of the caribou and reindeer forms a thick coat 2 inches thick. Each hair has a cylindrical cavity full of air that makes the fur light and insulating. In late spring they lose a large part of their fur, making them look rather ragged.

Reindeer and caribou are not the only animals that change appearance and habits with the arrival of summer. The days have grown longer and longer, and finally the June and July sun melts the upper layer of soil, permitting water to penetrate to the roots of the plants. With the buds they formed the previous summer fully developed, the flowers react to the warmth and moisture and bloom profusely. The first plant to flower in the Arctic is always the saxifrage. Insects and other tiny forms of animal life awaken with the flowers, and millions of caterpillars attack the vegetation and provide abundant food for the birds. First the mosquitoes and a month later the sand flies leave the ponds in impressive swarms, and spiders, plant lice, worms and beetles invade the earth. Wasps buzz ceaselessly and, incredibly, reach the extreme north of Greenland at a latitude of 83°.

In July, geese, ducks and waders brood their eggs, and their nestlings are often decimated by foxes and birds of prey. In the lakes, pike also prey upon small fish. The snow owls, gyrfalcons and peregrine falcons swoop down upon lemmings and voles, while weasels and ermines hunt hares and ground squirrels. Despite the incessant predation at every level, summer in the tundra may appear almost idyllic, and one may meet wolves, comfortably full after eating some small prey, wandering peacefully among the caribou, who graze without giving them a glance.

In August and September weather on the tundra is stable, and the assault of the mosquitoes and sand flies that have tormented both humans and animals for three months finally abates. This is another time of abundance, with a large quantity of ripe berries full of vitamins. Birds and mammals, including wolves and foxes, which are

204-205 *The Arctic fox, unlike its furtive, suspicious southern cousin, the red fox, is curious and invasive, and many researchers and travelers have been able to approach them and offer them food. Guided by its keen sense of smell, the Arctic fox can slip into a camp in search of excitement, heedless of human presence. It is not even afraid of polar bears, and will wait at a distance until this giant finishes its meal so it can feed on the leftovers. The Arctic fox is an excellent and tireless hunter, feeding on lemmings, voles and Arctic hares.*

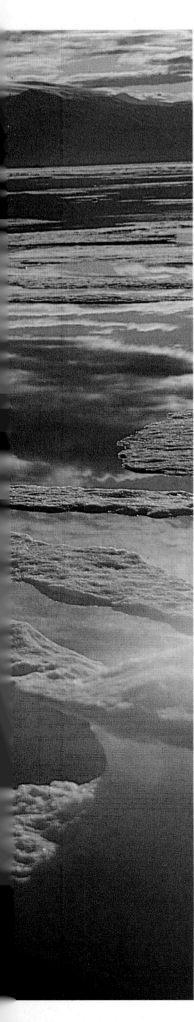

normally carnivores, fill up on blueberries, bearberries, cassiope berries and marsh myrtle.

At the bottom of the ponds the larvae of mosquitoes and other insects bury themselves in the mud, where they will remain until next spring. The plants produce buds which will be ready to flower the next year. The exodus of birds provides an even more spectacular sight than their arrival. Indeed, in mid-autumn they rise up into flocks that can blot out the sky. Many sedentary animals take on a white color that will continue until late next spring. The only true hibernating species on the tundra, the ground squirrel and the marmot, have already retreated into their dens. Within a couple of weeks the lakes and ponds will be covered with ice, the first snow will fall and each day the coastal ice will extend a little farther into the sea.

Having completed the annual cycle of life in the Arctic, capable of transforming a silent desert into a bursting show of life for several months, we should take a closer look at the true protagonists of the Nordic summer, those millions of migratory birds that have chosen the Arctic as a place to mate and nest. Migratory birds are for the most part aquatic, both pelagic and coastal. They represent 90% of the migratory flow, and of them, half nest on inaccessible coasts or uninhabited islands. Nests on sheer cliffs are quite primitive: the females lay the eggs, which have one very pointed end to prevent them from rolling, on a small shelf of rock and brood them right there, with no shelter or protection.

Pelagic birds always have palmate toes and dive into the sea using a variety of techniques, each one typical of that family. Some dive with their wings pressed close to their bodies, entering the water like a bullet; some dive deep by using their wings like fins; and some turn upside down in the water and reach food with their long necks. Other birds like swans, geese, loons, ducks and phalaropes nest on flat land either on the coast or inland, in the latter case building a true nest. Finally, the waders, although they should be considered aquatic because they live in and feed from the water, do not have palmate toes, but long legs and beaks suitable for capturing their prey. These birds also build their nests on the ground.

The great variety of birds that nest in northern regions can best be described by dividing them into orders. Some typical representatives of summer Arctic birdlife belong to the Procellariidae family (of the Procellariiformes order). They include the northern fulmar (*Fulmaris glacialis*), which is very similar to a seagull, but larger. Like the seagull it has the habit of rummaging through garbage. It can be distinguished from sea gulls by the noticeable tubular nostrils on the beak and its more rigid, often flat flying pattern. It nests on inaccessible cliffs. The stormy petrel (*Hydrobates pelagicus*) is a rather small bird which tends to skim the water's surface among high waves. It nests on the cliffs. Leach's petrel (*Oceanodroma leucorrhoa*) is larger than the former. When it flies, it does not skim the waves, but stays a certain distance from the sea, beating its wings in a butterfly-like manner.

The Manx shearwater (*Puffinus puffinus*) is the smallest of the shearwaters, and gathers in flocks both at sea and during nesting on the cliffs. The sooty shearwater (*Puffinus griseus*) is larger than the former and is coastal rather than pelagic.

The family of pelicans and related species (the Pelecaniformes order) includes large birds, of which only gannets and cormorants live in the Arctic. The gannet (*Sula bassana*) is an elegant, impressive bird. It builds a well-constructed nest with dried algae and twigs on a smooth platform not too far above sea level. The gannet nests on islands and cliffs, where it can protect the nest from land predators, primarily foxes, leaving the most impervious walls to the seagulls and members of the Alcidae family. Gannets reach the highest latitudes in the northern part of Baffin Bay.

The great cormorant (*Phalacrocorax carbo*) is also large and is a true specialist in underwater fishing. It does not venture to high latitudes and rarely into the open sea. It nests in malodorous colonies not far from the seashore. The shag (*Phalacrocorax aristotelis*) greatly resembles the cormorant. It can be distinguished by the tuft above the eyes and its smaller size. Like the cormorant, the shag wets its feather before diving so it will not float, and after eating spends long periods in the sun drying itself.

The seagulls, terns, and jaegers all belong to the Charadriiformes order, which includes the Laridae and Stercoraridae families. The many

varieties of seagulls have proved most adaptable to all kinds of habitat and food. Two factors have contributed to extending their territory northward: their ability to live near humans and the gradual rise in temperatures in the Arctic. Many seagulls live near canning factories, and they follow fishing boats, frequent ports and gather in the thousands near dumps. Only the Sabine's gull, the Ross' gull, the Iceland gull and the ivory gull are Arctic species; the others tend to remain farther south.

The ivory gull *(Pagophila eburnea)* is the smallest of the seagulls. It is completely white with black feet and a black beak, and flies as elegantly as the tern. It feeds on plankton that it pecks from the surface without entering the water, but like all seagulls it also acts as a trash collector, feeding on any kind of refuse.

The Sabine's gull *(Xenia sabini)* inhabits more northerly territories and islands. In the summer it feeds on insects and spiders, while it spends the winter on the open sea, where it feeds on pelagic animals. The Ross' gull *(Rhodosthethia rosea)* lives in Arctic Asia and can be distinguished by its pale pink color, with a narrow black band around the neck. Its wings are white and its tail is forked rather than fan-shaped. In the summer it feeds on food it finds in the lakes, while in the winter it eats what the sea offers.

The Iceland gull *(Larus glaucoides)* is as large as the herring gull but has no black on its wings. In its second winter of life it is pure white. It gathers with both herring gulls and glaucous gulls.

The herring gull *(Larus argentatus)* is the most common of all seagulls. Highly adaptive to any climate and any kind of food, it is common in ports, near garbage dumps and by rivers and lakes. It nests on cliffs, uninhabited islands and isolated coasts. In addition to human leavings, the herring gull feeds on bivalve mollusks, breaking their shells by dropping them onto the rocks. The glaucous gull *(Larus hyperboreus)* is a large bird with a wingspan of 50 feet. It is also white during its second year of life.

The glaucous gull can be distinguished from other gulls by its distinctly predatory habits: it steals eggs and kills nestlings and even adult birds. In the winter it feeds on plankton at lower latitudes. The great black-backed gull *(Larus marinus)* is as large as the glaucous gull, but with dark gray wings.

It is also predatory. The lesser black-backed gull *(Larus fuscus)* is a little smaller than the herring gull, which it resembles. Its plumage is more like the great black-backed gull. Its beak and feet are bright yellow, and it is very common along the coasts and near ports at high latitudes.

The black-legged kittiwake *(Rissa tridactyla)* is a pelagic species which never comes close to the coast except to nest in large colonies on the steep cliffs. It has characteristic short feet and an elegant flight, almost like a tern. The mew gull *(Larus canus)* is the same size as the black-legged kittiwake, but its legs and beak are greenish in color. It inhabits a vast area. Its beak is thinner than other seagulls, allowing it to catch worms and insect larvae. In the winter it can be seen on more southerly coasts.

208-209 The timber wolf (Canis lupis arctos) lives on Ellesmere Island, the northernmost island in the Canadian archipelago. Its coat remains white all year round and consists of an outer coat of longer, stiffer hairs and a very dense, woolly undercoat which is shed in the summer. The wolf is an affectionate father and faithful mate who helps his companion raise their young and teach them how to hunt. On Ellesmere Island its prey are musk oxen, Pary caribou and other smaller mammals. Hunting timber wolves is now prohibited, even for the Inuit.

The Arctic tern *(Sterna paradisaea)* is the only tern that lives in the northern hemisphere, where it nests on the tundra. It is common from northern Alaska to the Canadian archipelago, from Greenland to many polar islands and throughout Arctic Eurasia. This tern is perhaps the most beautiful bird of the North, with a soft gray plumage, silvery white tail and wings, coral colored beak and feet and a black head. In June it comes to the eastern hemisphere and, without even building a nest, lays its eggs among the gravel or dry grass. If there is danger, the whole colony mobilizes to protect the eggs. Between August and September even the newly hatched fledglings are capable of flying south, sometimes reaching lands at the edge of the Antarctic ice pack. These small, delicate birds make this long voyage twice a year, for a total of about 10,000 miles, with very few casualties. The tern dives into the sea a bit awkwardly, fishing from the surface.

The great skua *(Stercorarius skua) resembles* the herring gull, but is darker and larger. The skua is a rather cruel bird that not only eats fish and plankton caught in the sea, but also attacks the parents of other smaller species as they are regurgitating food for their nestlings, taking it and destroying the nests to scatter the nestlings, which it eats. It does not disdain carrion either. It nests in colonies on the tundra not far from the sea.

The parasitic jaeger *(Stercorarius parasiticus)* is the most common of the species. It is somewhat smaller but is equally prone to attacking other birds, especially terns, to take away what they have in their mouths. Like the great skua, it nests in small colonies on the tundra, preying on both small mammals and fish. The long-tailed jaeger *(Stercorarius longicaudus)* is the smallest of the species and is less prone to plunder other marine birds. It also has a graceful flight similar to the tern. The long-tailed jaeger feeds on lemmings and voles in the summer and on fish in the winter.

The large Charadriiformes order also includes the Alcidae family: all members are distinguished by their white and black plumage.

Four species of the Alcidae family live in Arctic waters: great auks, guillemots, razorbills and puffins. They should be considered the northern hemisphere's counterpart to penguins. Like penguins, they use their short, narrow wings to swim underwater with great skill. Unlike their southern cousins, they can fly by beating their

wings very rapidly, making a noise that from close up almost sounds like buzzing. They feed exclusively on fish, and the larger species dive into the water to depths of up to over 300 feet.

The razorbill *(Alca torda)* nests in colonies on the cliffs, sometimes together with guillemots, but in general not on such steep rocks. With its white breast and black back, it could be mistaken for a guillemot, which is about the same size. The razorbill can be distinguished by the form of its beak and its stubbier neck. The guillemot or common murre *(Uria algae)* nests in colonies on steep cliffs, and like the razorbill spends the winter in the sea. It can be distinguished from the thick-billed murre or Brünnich guillemot by

the white stripe near the eye that runs to the head. It skims the water in linear formations.

The thick-billed murre or Brünnich guillemot *(Uria lomvia)* is the same size as the common murre and can be distinguished by its shorter beak. It has the same color plumage and nests on steep rocks. The black guillemot *(Cepphus grylle)* nests alone or in colonies on rocks sheer to the sea. Unlike the other members of the Alcidae family mentioned above, which have black feet, this species has bright red feet. It also reaches higher latitudes than other guillemots. The little auk *(Plautus alle)* is about half the height of the other species and has a very short neck and beak. It skims the water in linear formations, beating its wings very rapidly. It nests on cliffs sheer to

the sea and is more pelagic than the other members of the Alcidae family. Eskimos catch many little auks with nets.

The puffin *(Fratercula arctica)* nests on the highest cliffs, and in the winter is pelagic. It is the most colorful member of the Alcidae family, with orange feet and a large orange, parrot-like bill. In the winter the beak usually loses its most colorful outer layers, which return in the spring. This species is also hunted by Eskimos, in this case with the aid of a quite singular dog known as the lundehund or puffinhound, the only dog in the world which has six toes on each foot. With its extraordinary grip on the rocks, it can reach and catch puffins.

The swans, some of the showiest and most elegant of all birds, are members of the Anseriformes order, the Anatidae family and the Cygnidae subfamily. There are only two species of Arctic swans. One is the whistling swan *(Cygnus cygnus)*, which has a particular whistling call as it flies. It comes to the lakes and ponds of the tundra in June and always returns to last year's nest. It is pure white with a black beak with a yellow base. Its legs are gray black. The other species is the Bewick's tundra swan *(Cygnus bewickii)*, which is smaller than the whistling swan. While the whistling swan comes from North American, the Bewick's swan reaches the Arctic from Eurasia.

The geese are also members of the Anseriformes order (to which they give the name), the Anatidae family and the Anserinae sub-family. All these birds are large, strong fliers. Their plumage varies widely and is the same for both sexes. Geese migrate north each year in large, noisy flocks and reproduce in the cold lands of the Canadian tundra, Greenland or Arctic Siberia. All nest on the ground near freshwater lakes and ponds and ferociously defend their nests. They feed on seedlings, tender leaves and algae. Geese fly in a characteristic V formation.

Following is a list of the species present in the Arctic and their nesting areas:
Snow goose *(Anser hyperboreus)*: the tundra in Alaska and northern Canada
Brent goose *(Branta bernicla)*: Greenland and the Svalbards

211 top There are two varieties of Arctic lemmings: the collared lemming (Dicrostonyx groenlandicus) and the brown lemming (Lemmus trimucronatus). The former is the Eurasian variety, while the latter is the North American one. The lemming is the first link in the food chain for a multitude of predators. As it is quite common on the tundra, it is the preferred prey for all carnivorous mammals and raptors.

212 A gyrfalcon (Falcus rusticolus) was photographed on the Kent Peninsula on the Canadian mainland. This is the largest species of falcon and has a completely white body, with brown spots on its wings. It preys on Arctic hares, lemmings and voles. It is a faithful partner to the female, which is larger than the male.

212-213 A pair of snow owls (Nyctea scandiaca) was photographed near their nest on the tundra. The male is carrying a lemming, which the female, larger and more spotted, gladly accepts. The number of snow owls varies according to a multi-year cycle that follows the lemming population. In good years more eggs are hatched, while the owls lay fewer eggs when lemmings are scarce.

Red-necked goose *(Branta ruficollis)*: Greenland and the Svalbards

Barnacle goose *(Branta leucopsis)*: Greenland, the Svalbards and Novaya Zemlya

White-fronted goose *(Anser albifrons)*: marshy areas throughout the Arctic

Bean goose *(Anser fabalis)*: Iceland and marshy areas in the Eurasian tundra

Pink-footed goose *(Anser brachyrhynchus)*: Iceland and marshy area in the Eurasian tundra

Canada goose *(Branta canadensis)* marshy areas throughout the Arctic

The loons belong to the Gaviformes order and the Gavidae family and have very retracted legs, which makes their movements quite powerful. These birds are perfectly adapted to swimming and diving, are fast and powerful fliers and are only a little smaller than geese. Their beaks are more pointed than swans, geese or ducks. They feed on fish, crustaceans and aquatic plants. In the summer the males' plumage is exceptionally beautiful.

Arctic loon *(Gavia arctica)*

Red-throated loon *(Gavia stellata)*

Common loon *(Gavia immer)*

Yellow-billed loon *(Gavia adamsi)*

The sea ducks are also part of the great Anseriformes order and the large Anatidae family. They belong to the Aythynae subfamily. About 20 species of duck live in the Arctic, and over half of them spend their lives in the sea. Some are purely marine, nesting and wintering along the beaches. The eiders belong to this group:

Common eider *(Somateria mollissima)*

Spectacled eider *(Arctonecta fischeri)*

King eider *(Somateria spectabilis)*

Steller's eider *(Polysticta stelleri)*

Humans have always sought these birds, as the down from their breast is the most valuable natural material in the world for stuffing pillows, featherbeds and down jackets.

Other ducks prefer to live inland on rivers and lakes during the summer and return to the sea or river estuaries in the winter. Some of these include:

Harlequin duck *(Histrionicus histrionicus)*

Common goldeneye *(Bucephala clangula)*

Common merganser *(Mergus merganser)*

Red-breasted merganser (Mergus serrator)

Velvet scoter *(Melanitta fusca)*

Black scoter *(Melanitta nigra)*

Oldsquaw *(Clangula hymemalis)*

Freshwater ducks also belong to the Anseriformes order and the Anatidae family. These ducks are all smaller than marine ducks. Large colonies of ducks live near freshwater as well, although there are not as many species as marine ducks. Many of these birds are well known in our latitudes, where they come to winter. Some of them include:

Mallard *(Anas platyrhincus)*

Northern pintail *(Anas acuta)*

Gadwall *(Anas strepera)*

Baikal teal *(Anas formosa)*

Blue-winged teal *(Anas discors)*

Eurasian wild widgeon *(Anas penelope)*

In addition to loons and freshwater ducks, there is a very large family that frequents nearly the same territories in the tundra: the waders. These birds have very long legs, non-palmate toes and long, thin beaks with forms that vary from species to species. This diversity allows

213 top *A snowy owl approaches its prey silently, thanks to its very flexible flight feathers. This raptor is protected by dense plumage even on its claws and has no external auricular tufts. An eyelid, not present in other owls, protects it from snow blindness. Its plumage is perennially white.*

214 top   A barnacle goose (Branta leucopsis) photographed in the Svalbard Islands, rises from the water in flight. The barnacle goose has different habits from the many other species of geese in the Arctic, and rather than nesting on the tundra, it builds its nests in mountain areas where it is protected from foxes.

them to peacefully coexist with different kinds of birds in the same place, as they each have a different niche. One of the most important and numerous is the sandhill crane *(Grus canadensis)*, the giant of migrating waders. It builds a very sturdy nest of dry grass, surrounded by water on all sides. It is iron-gray in color and can be distinguished from the American crane by its color (the American crane is white) and its smaller size. It belongs to the Gruiformes order. Other important waders include:

Eurasian curlew *(Numenius arquata)*
Whimbrel *(Numenius phaeopus)*
Black-tailed godwit *(Limosa limosa)*
Bar-tailed godwit *(Limosa lapponica)*
Red knot *(Calidris canutus)*
Dunlin *(Calidris alpina)*
Violet sandpiper *(Calidris maritima)*
Sanderling *(Calidris alba)*
Black-bellied plover *(Pluvialis squatarola)*
European golden plover *(Pluvialis apricaria)*
Greater golden plover *(Pluvialis dominica)*
Dotterel *(Eudromias morinellus)*
Ruddy turnstone *(Arenaria interpres)*
Green sandpiper *(Tringa ochropus)*
Wood sandpiper *(Tringa glareola)*
Common redshank *(Tringa totanus)*
Ruff *(Philomacus pugnax)*
Little stint *(Calidris minuta)*
Common ringed plover *(Charadrius hiaticula)*
Palearctic oystercatcher *(Haematopus ostralegus)*

With the exception of the crane, all these birds belong to the Charadriiformes order and the two families of Charadriidae and Haematopodidae. They live in colonies and nest near ponds or rivers or along the seacoast. They lay their eggs on the ground and hide them among low vegetation. They feed on small fish, crustaceans, worms and other invertebrates. The phalaropes are quite similar in appearance to the preceding birds, except that they have shorter legs and lobed (not palmate) toes, which permit them to swim with some proficiency. They nest on coastal lagoons and often swim in circles in the water to stir up food. Unlike ducks and waders, the females are larger and more colorful than the males. They also belong to the Charadriidae family.

214-215 The image shows a great flock of geese during a migratory flight. This American species flies from the Great Lakes region to Arctic Canada in a single voyage of 1,800 miles. There is also a very rare blue-gray variety of this bird which has a white head and neck.

215 top The snow goose (Anser hyperboreus) gathers in large numbers in the marshes before taking flight. This species

frequents the American continent and is rarely seen in Europe. It nests in the tundra and is unmistakable due to its pure white plumage with black flight feathers.

215 bottom The Arctic tern (Sterna paradisea) is not only an elegant bird, but it also holds the record for long-distance migration. In fact, this bird spends the summer in the Arctic and the winter in the Antarctic, migrating twice a year up to 4,500-5,000 miles.

The following species are common in the Arctic:

Wilson's phalarope *(Phalaropus tricolor)*
Red phalarope *(Phalaropus fulicarius)*
Red-necked phalarope *(Phalarope lobatus)*

After discussing the numerous aquatic migratory birds, we should at least mention the land birds which migrate to the North in the summer. We have seen how the diversified morphology of the Arctic territories offers a vast range of nesting possibilities for aquatic birds. The rugged coast offers both a safe refuge for pelagic birds that nest on the cliffs or at least lay their eggs there, and an immense flat territory scattered with millions of large and small lakes and ponds, providing nesting areas for the most diverse families of non-pelagic migrating birds.

The Arctic tundra offers shelter for the following non-aquatic birds:

Snow bunting *(Plectrophenax nivalis)*
Yellowhammer *(Emberiza citronella)*
Lapland longspur *(Calcarius lapponichus)*
Northern wheatear *(Oenanthe oenanthe)*

These songbirds are the harbingers of spring, and their songs echo across the still empty tundra of early spring. Because they feed on seeds and berries which they find under the snow, they can arrive before other birds that must wait for insects and spiders to appear after the thaw. Some of the most important include:

Bluethroat *(Luscinia svecica)*
Water pipet *(Anthus spinoletta)*
Eastern water pipet *(Anthus spinoletta littoralis)*
Meadow pipet *(Anthus pratensis)*
Red-throated pipet *(Anthus corvinus)*
White wagtail *(Motacilla alba alba)*
Yellow wagtail *(Motacilla citreola)*
Redwing *(Turdus iliacus)*
Fieldfare *(Turdus pilaris)*

All these birds catch insects on the ground and in the shrubs, while the following two species catch insects while flying:

Horned skylark *(Eremophila alpestris)*
Sand martin or bank swallow *(Riparia riparia)*

There are very few raptors in the Arctic. In compensation, they have more prey available than in southern latitudes. Raptors include the snow owl and the gyrfalcon, which have already been described under the sedentary birds, plus two other falcons that can be seen in the Arctic

216 center *The razorbill* (Alca torda) *is also very common throughout the Arctic. Like the guillemot, it nests in large colonies on rocks sheer to the sea and feeds by diving into the water and skillfully catching fish. Like the guillemot, it beats its wings very rapidly and noisily.*

216 bottom *The puffin* (Fraterculus arctica) *is the most colorful of the sea birds that migrate to the Arctic. Its beak is large and showy, and in the summer the tip becomes a red-orange color which disappears in the winter. It has the largest head of all members of the great auk family, which makes it recognizable both in flight and on the rocks. It often comes to its nest with numerous little fish in its beak, which gives it a quite amazing appearance. The tuft of golden feathers at the back of its head, its red-rimmed eyes and its claws the same color as its beak, contribute to its rather clownish appearance.*

217 *Hundreds of gannets* (Sula bassana) *nest on the Herna Ness cliffs at the far northern edge of the Shetland Islands. This large bird, bigger than a goose, has an extremely wide territory which in the summer reaches the northern area of Baffin Bay. The gannet is a member of the pelican family, and like the pelican it catches fish by diving into the water from a height of 30-45 feet, or by swimming underwater.*

218 A male caribou
finds winter shelter in the
sub-arctic territory of
Alaska. The snow has just
fallen in Denali
National Park (Denali is
the Inuit name for
Mount McKinley, the
highest peak in North
America). Here the
caribou are safe from
hunters, but in the spring
their instinct leads them
out of the park
northward, in search of a
cooler climate.

219 A herd of caribou was photographed while, during the spring migration north to the Brooks Range in northern Alaska, parts of the ground are still covered with snow. It is hard for the caribou to find food: they use their hooves to dig into the frozen snow in search of a few tufts of Cladonia, their favorite lichen.

220-221 *The caribou* (Rangifer tarandus) *is an animal typical of the American Arctic. At one time it numbered in the millions, but over the past two centuries it has been decimated, and now there are only about a million caribou left in Canada and Alaska. Unlike the reindeer, its* Eurasian cousin, the *caribou has never been domesticated and is hunted in the wild by several Inuit populations, for whom it provides the main means of sustenance. This deer makes two migrations a year, one in the spring northward, in search of tundra lichens and a cooler climate, and* one in the autumn, when *it returns to the taiga with its trees that provide shelter from the frigid north winds. Caribou shed their antlers each year. The new ones are covered with a velvety skin rich in blood vessels, which helps the animal disperse excessive heat. In the autumn they shed this skin* and the antlers assume *another function: autumn is the rutting season, and males engage in furious body-to-body combat, attempting to gore their adversary with the sharp ends of their uncovered antlers. The antlers are then shed in early winter and grow back the next spring.*

during the summer. The peregrine falcon *(Falco peregrinus)* is smaller than the gyrfalcon, but has the same predatory habits and very similar plumage during the summer. The merlin *(Falco columbarius)* is much smaller than other falcons and has more narrow, pointed wings, which makes its flight distinguishable from other species. Sometimes large raptors like the golden eagle *(Aquila chyrsaëtos)*, whose habitat is on the higher elevations of the tundra, move up to Arctic territories, attracted by the abundant prey, while the bald eagle *(Haliaëetos leucocephalus)* makes its habitat on the opposite shores of Alaska and eastern Siberia. Finally, the white-tailed sea-eagle *(Haliëetus albicilla)* can be found on the sea coast and larger lakes.

All the animals described to this point are habitual sedentary or migratory species in the Arctic. But the tundra also has numerous occasional visitors. Some of the animals who occasionally frequent the Arctic during the summer include the grizzly bear *(Ursus horribilus)*, which appears in the spring to feed on seedlings and tender leaves, gorges on salmon in the summer and prepares for hibernation by filling up on any kind of edible berry in the fall. The timber wolf *(Canis lupus)* comes out of the forests following the caribou migrations. It attacks young or weak animals. The coyote *(Canis latrans)* is another versatile animal capable of adapting to any type of terrain or climate. It feeds on small tundra mammals but does not disdain carrion left by wolves and bears.

The red fox *(Vulpes fulva)* has extended its territory a few degrees of latitude north over the past 100 years and is greatly increasing in the Arctic. The wolverine *(Gulus luscus)* is the largest animal in the mustelid family and has unequaled courage and ferocity. It can intimidate any animal, including the wolf, and may even kill young caribou.

The Dali sheep *(Ovis dalli)*, with its white coat and large horns similar to those of the European mouflon, comes down from the mountains in search of food, then quickly retreats to cliffs inaccessible to wolves.

The mountain goat *(Oreamnos americanus)* sometimes comes down from the impregnable mountains in which it lives when bad weather forces it to find food at lower elevations. The

snowshoe hare *(Lepus americanus)* may be confused with the Arctic hare, because its fur becomes white in the winter. In the summer it is brownish red. It has larger feet than the Arctic species, as it snows much more where it usually lives than in the extreme Arctic.

The muskrat *(Ondatra zibethica)* resembles a small beaver, but has a cylindrical tail and a more bristly coat. It builds dens on the water with materials that can be eaten when food becomes scarce. Its fur is sought after, but despite its numerous enemies, the greatest of which is man, its high rate of reproduction protects it from any danger of extinction.

Unlike the other animals listed above, which venture into Arctic territories in the summer, the Canadian lynx *(Lynx canadensis)* makes its incursions to the tundra in the winter and spring, when the game in the forests where it usually lives is depleted. Its favorite prey is the Arctic hare and the snowshoe hare. The river otter *(Lutra canadensis)* has summer habits. It is smaller than the sea otter and is the species most adaptable to any type of habitat, provided it is near fresh water. It is also more versatile in its eating habits, and will feed on crustaceans, mollusks, fish, frogs, snails and insects.

The sea otter *(Enhydra lutris)* is common on the western coasts of Alaska and the Aleutian Islands. It feeds on fish, mollusks and sea urchins and in the past was ruthlessly hunted for its valuable fur. Currently a protected species, it is estimated that 30,000-40,000 sea otters now exist.

A polar bear slowly walks on the ice-pack illuminated by the light of the setting sun. This massive, solitary creature, capable of dominating a most hostile, wild environment, is a symbol of the entire Arctic, of its beauty and immensity.

ILLUSTRATION CREDITS